Teach the ESSENTIAL
GOOD CHARACTER with

Paul Cicchini

RESEARCH PRESS
PUBLISHERS

2612 North Mattis Avenue ■ Champaign, Illinois 61822 ■ [800] 519-2707 ■ www.researchpress.com

RESEARCH PRESS
PUBLISHERS

5 4 3 2 1 19 20 21 22 23

The slide show for use with this book and the bingo worksheets (found in Appendix A) are available for free download on the book webpage at **www.researchpress.com/downloads**

Copies of this book may be ordered from Research Press at the address given on the title page.

Composition by Jeff Helgesen
Illustrations by Alexis Green, Opik, and Jason Cicchini
Cover design by Linda Brown, Positive I.D. Graphic Design, Inc.
Printed by Seaway Printing

ISBN 978-0-87822-718-1
Library of Congress Control Number 2019943572

Thank you to my wife, Susan, for being my sounding board and my biggest cheerleader.

Thank you to Dr. Maurice Elias for mentoring me and showing me that what I wanted to teach kids was an actual thing, and it was called Social Emotional Learning.

Thanks to all the editors at Research Press, but a special thank you to Elizabeth Hess for respecting my work and guiding my vision.

Thank you to my dad, Chick Cicchini, for being the quiet, hard-working man of good character that was my inspiration in choosing the right path.

Contents

1

Overview: The Need for Character Education

Does this scenario sound familiar? You sign in to work at school in the morning, get your classroom ready for the day's lessons, go out to your morning duty station in the hallway and start talking to a colleague. Boom! The doors open up, and students come streaming in. Several of the students walk in between you and your colleague or practically knock you over without an "excuse me," a "good morning" or any other acknowledgment of your existence. You feel annoyed and wonder where these children acquired such abominable manners.

Or this one? It's time to collect homework in your fifth period class, and nearly a third of your students shrug and say to you, "I don't have it," or "I didn't do it." You want to do a full-on 'face-palm' right then and there because your school has a free afterschool homework club as well a silent sustained reading period built into the schedule when homework can be accomplished prior to going home. Why can't your students take ownership of their single most important responsibility?

What counselor or school psychologist hasn't witnessed this? During your lunchtime walk-through of the cafeteria where you touch base with students, you observe a bigger boy picking on another boy—the quiet one from one of your counseling groups who does his schoolwork but doesn't seem to have a lot of friends. The bigger one is ridiculing the clothes/looks/speech of the other one. Bystander students begin to take notice but don't intervene. You instantly do something to shut this down before the victim experiences any more emotional scars. If you teach in New Jersey, for example, you are obligated to file a HIB (Harassment, Intimidation & Bullying) report on the offending student, but how do you prevent the problem before it even starts? How do you change your school's culture so that everyone knows that bullying is not tolerated?

If any or all of these scenarios sound familiar, this book is for you.

Unfortunately, some educators believe that I am preaching to the choir by training educators how to teach good manners, responsibility and tolerance to their students. "If parents only raised their children better," some teachers say, "I wouldn't have to worry about these issues. I could stick to my job of teaching math, English, science, and so on and be more effective."

My response to that mindset is if we want to see a change, we have to be the agent of change. We can no longer assume or rely on parents to effectively instill prosocial behavior in their children. A 1997 study by clinical psychologists showed that ineffective parenting was related to conduct problems of children who were low in callousness traits (Wootton, Frick, Shelton, & Silverthorn, 1997), and in turn, children that scored high on callousness traits showed a lack of empathy towards others, regardless of parenting styles.

Many people believe that parents are more reluctant students than our school-age students, so perhaps parent education programs and the hope for trickle-down to our students is not the most effective strategy. No, it seems that it is up to us to impart lessons on proper behavior, manners, and good citizenship directly to our students. If teachers don't teach these skills, a child might not have anyone else in their lives that will.

Therein lies the true value of character education. It almost seems self-explanatory, but if we formally define character education, it is the teaching of the benefits and virtues of adopting those human traits that are almost universally considered as "good" as well as skills that help humans get along with each other in a structured society. These "good traits" can be described as the core values we all need to have in order to cooperate and keep our civilization running smoothly.

Thomas Lickona described it as this: "Character Education is a deliberate effort to cultivate virtue.... It is not an add-on...it is a whole-school effort to create a community of virtue...where behaviors such as respect, honesty, kindness, hard work and self-control are promoted explicitly, modeled, taught, expected, celebrated, and continuously practiced in everyday actions" (Lickona, 1994). Another description is adapted from Lickona's Why Character Matters: "Character education is the constellation of virtues, or objectively good human qualities a person possesses" (Lickona, 2004).

Character education was actually an accepted part of the curriculum in our schools well over a century ago. The founding fathers of the United States realized that having people who learned to respect others and valued fairness and honesty was essential to the survival of our growing democratic society. Character education is still valued by our government today. In fact, teaching core character values is one of the six key goals of the United States Department of Education: Develop safe schools and strong character (U.S. Department of Education, 2002).

If it is so prized by the U.S. Department of Education, why are so many American schools no longer teaching it or emphasizing it? The culprit seems to be a lack of proper school funding. Here is the domino effect that unfairly impacts the efficacy of schools: when the economy suffers a downturn (as we experienced in this country from 2007 to 2009), voters complain to their elected officials about taxes, and they threaten to pull their support in the next election. Politicians want to stay in office, so they respond to this outcry with a knee-jerk reaction: they refuse to raise taxes (even on businesses or the rich) enough to keep up with inflation, or they even cut taxes. As you may have guessed, when taxes are cut or remain flat, there is less money to fund public education. This loss of federal and state aid for schools creates a seemingly never-ending round of school budget cuts. One of the first things to get slashed (along with the arts) is character education.

However, very few people realize that the above sequence is counterintuitive. Character education should be one of the last areas to suffer cuts, because not only do character education programs pay for themselves, they in fact provide an overall cost-saving measure for schools. A study by the Josephson Institute of Ethics on the effectiveness of one character education program was done in 2007 (Josephson Institute, 2007). In one case study, the Institute found that reports of bullying were reduced by 86 percent as a result of that character education program.

Another case study reported by Josephson on the Downey Unified School District in California indicated that in the three years prior to any proposed character education interventions being implemented, the total number of suspension days rose from 5,582 to 6,417, an increase of 14.96 percent. However, in the four years after a specific character education intervention, the total number of suspension days decreased from 6,417 to 3,757, a decrease of 41.45 percent. If we have fewer suspensions, we spend less money on home instruction. If we have fewer fights in school, we could spend less on security staff, and our teachers would feel safer as well. With less staff turnover, we save on recruiting and new teacher training. Finally, if we have students in special education programs that are socially/emotionally competent (a major objective of character education), the students could better manage their own behavior. They are more likely to remain in-district instead of being placed in expensive private specialized schools. With all these savings in so many areas, there would be more money to fund our schools and even to hire more teachers. With more teachers, we keep the teacher-to-student ratio low—which, as studies show, is a key component to teacher effectiveness.

There is still more convincing evidence in the case for character education. Short-sighted politicians often point to standardized test scores as proof that our public schools are ineffective and that we are falling behind the rest of the world in educational effectiveness. In 2008, the Collaborative for Academic, Social, and Emotional Learning (CASEL) conducted a meta-analysis of social emotional learning and character education program effectiveness. Across all studies, there was an 11 percent gain in standardized scores (Payton, 2008).

The following are highlights of an executive summary of a survey published by the highly regarded journal, Education Week:

- To better understand educators' views of social and emotional learning, the Education Week Research Center invited users of edweek.org—Education Week's website to participate in an online survey in April 2015 (Blad, 2015).
- 562 qualified K–12 teachers/school-based administrators responded.
- The respondents represented a wide range of grade levels, experience, and school settings.
- Slightly more than one in three respondents reported that they were very familiar with social and emotional learning.
- Self-management was the social and emotional trait rated most important for students to learn, while respondents perceived that responsible decision-making was the trait that was most important for teachers to possess.
- Fourteen percent of respondents indicated that more than three-quarters of students in their schools had strong social and emotional skills.
- Just fewer than half the respondents said that social and emotional learning received too little attention.
- Among survey respondents whose schools were implementing the Common Core State Standards, the majority (59 percent) said the amount of attention paid to students' social and emotional learning had remained the same since the implementation of the standards.
- The most prevalent social and emotional learning challenge facing educators was that other issues often take priority, leaving limited time to focus on this area.
- Many respondents (57 percent) indicated that their educator preparation programs had not adequately prepared them to address students' social and emotional learning. However, most (63 percent also indicated that they had received sufficient

training and professional development after obtaining certification as an educator.)

Study after study (available on the CASEL website) shows that when you have emotionally and socially competent students, discipline and bullying referrals go down and test scores and graduation rates go up.

2

The Basics of Character Education and Social–Emotional Learning

There are several other highly-structured, fairly well-organized Character Education programs available to teachers and counselors. They have some variation, but for the most part, they focus on the same set of core values:

1. Respect/Manners
2. Honesty/Trustworthiness
3. Fairness/Justice
4. Responsibility/Accountability
5. Caring/Tolerance of Others
6. Good Citizenship

We will examine each one of these key values of good character.

1. ***Respect/Manners***. This aspect of good character includes saying "please," "excuse me," and "thank you," holding doors for others, avoiding foul language, and not interrupting conversations. It also includes observing the time-honored adage of "do unto others as you would have done unto you." Respect also means never using words to hurt, never resorting to physical aggression, and using positive conflict resolution skills. Above all, it means that when you do have a conflict with someone else, you endeavor to remember that they are a fellow human being, a person worthy of your respect.
2. ***Honesty/Trustworthiness***. This good character trait is exemplified by telling the truth, not cheating on tests, not taking things that don't belong to you, showing loyalty to family/friends/school, exhibiting reliability, and recognizing that your reputation is priceless and difficult to repair once it is damaged.
3. ***Fairness/Justice***. This quality means being a good sport, not cheating in competitions, playing fair and by the rules, sharing what you have with others, not judging others rashly, encouraging others to be fair, fighting for what is right, and advocating justice.
4. ***Responsibility/Accountability***. This means keeping your promises, doing your homework, studying, not blaming others for your actions, owning up to mistakes, thinking ahead to the consequences of your actions, having a sense of duty, and being a role model for your peers.
5. ***Caring/Tolerance of Others***. You can exemplify this trait by being accepting of others, not being a bully, trying to see things from someone else's point of view, practicing charity, serving others, being empathetic, and being thankful.
6. ***Good Citizenship***. This means understanding how our governments (national, state, local, school) work, obeying the law and the rules at school, respecting law enforcement officers, giving back to the community, being patriotic, and encouraging your family to vote and being involved in the democratic process.

In regards to the other professionally designed character education curriculums I mentioned above, a few are empirically based and some can be effective. However, nearly all of them are expensive. Teachers, counselors, and administrators have told me that they have paid upwards of $5,000 for character education programs! Some of the programs with a $1,000 price tag might be considered 'reasonably priced' if you are a large school district with a healthy budget. However, if you are a teacher or counselor from a small, underfunded district that has precious little discretionary funds, or if you wanted to buy a program like that on your own to avoid all the red tape, it's certainly not pocket change.

That is why this invaluable program is needed: to provide teachers, counselors, and school psychologists with an inexpensive way to incorporate the concepts of character education into their classroom in a way that is fun for students and faculty alike. Our hope is that our program is not only engaging, but dialogue-provoking as well.

Now that we know what topics character education covers, let's examine a fundamental principle behind character education: social emotional learning. For some people, it seems that being social comes naturally, and, indeed, some aspects of it are innate. However, social psychologists, especially in the 1960s, discovered that many social behaviors (either prosocial or antisocial) are learned. This social learning is accomplished either through conditioning (behavior that is rewarded or punished) or through modeling.

Albert Bandura is one of the most celebrated of these social psychologists. He designed field experiments to determine whether humans can learn behaviors by watching others, especially social behavior. In one very famous experiment, the 'Bobo the Clown' study, he showed how children between the ages of three and five could learn aggression simply by watching adults and peers model the behavior—in this case, punching a blow-up clown doll (Bandura, Ross, & Ross, 1961).

If you accept the finding of Bandura's research, then you understand that some people may have problems exhibiting prosocial behaviors because they either did not have good role models for the proper behavior or they lacked the opportunity at home or in their communities to practice the right kinds of social behaviors. If that is the case, I estimate that there could be potentially thousands of students that need to learn social interactions such as reading a person's body language or facial expressions, communicating effectively, and even feeling empathy for another because their home environments did not provide them with this.

If we consider social–emotional learning in addition to the six main topics of character education that I mentioned above, there are additional aspects of high character that are just as important to impress upon our children to make them socially healthy and emotionally resilient. The ones that I believe need stressing are:

- Self-control
- Confronting and overcoming fear
- Cooperation and teamwork
- The ability to forgive and the ability to seek forgiveness
- Personal integrity (a code of honor)
- Leadership

Self-control is important for our students because without it, learning becomes difficult, if not downright impossible. Delaying gratification, stretching your limits of attention and controlling your anger all fall under this category. I also like to point out to my students that besides facilitating learning, self-control (resisting the impulse to hit or blurt out whatever comes to mind) helps you make and keep friends.

I firmly believe that to achieve or accomplish anything worthwhile in life, you have to stare down the unknown. It may sound daunting, but you must have the courage to face it. We have to teach our children to not be paralyzed by fear. If we define courage as the ability to deal with fears, it is a priceless quality to teach our students so that they will not be afraid to ask questions, to be wrong, or to try something new. How else can learning take place?

The old saying goes, "Rome wasn't built in a day." It wasn't built with one set of hands either. It took people assuming different roles and working together. As much as we may have dreaded group projects in graduate school, it trained us in how to get along with others to get the job done. Big tasks require teamwork and cooperation, and for our society to continue humming along for generations to come, our students must learn that lesson, too.

We all mess up. Sometimes we mess up so colossally that we hurt others around us. If we don't summon the humility to ask for forgiveness, we will one day find ourselves alone. The same holds true for granting forgiveness to those that have hurt us. While it's important to teach our kids not to be emotional punching bags, it is equally important to send the message that everyone deserves a second chance. It's also vital that we, as adults, send the message that we recognize that when our students mess up, they deserve a second chance as well.

I believe that the concept of integrity is something that has been adulterated by popular culture and that has led to confusion for our children. They talk about "street cred" and "reputation" as being important to them. We need to help them clarify what's really valuable in that area. Their most prized possession should not be their "rep," per se, as much as it should be a more formalized, overall sense of personal integrity. Many definitions of integrity simply mention honesty, but I feel that it should refer more to a complete set of ethics. In earlier days, this concept was called a code of honor. We should be showing our students why it is important to have an honor code in schools. Furthermore, we should help them to develop their own code of honor for their lives outside of school. If they can follow a reliable moral compass that they have internalized, society will be the beneficiary.

Finally, we always implore our students to be leaders, but some of us don't know exactly what good leadership looks like. We say, "lead by example," but leadership is much more than that and we need to break down those qualities so that we can all agree on them and encourage them in our students.

In writing the fictional story about the Essentialz and creating this curriculum program, I have endeavored to not only include the six topics (as either a primary or secondary quality) that other programs do, but also the additional traits of social competence mentioned above because they are just as important and deserve equal consideration.

3

Holding Out for a Hero: Why Our Kids Connect with Superheroes

The very first time I had to counsel an elementary school student, I was paralyzed with indecision. "I can't just jump into their problems without establishing rapport," I thought, "they'll just shut right down on me!" I agonized over what I should talk to them about first. I knew how to talk to high schoolers. They were like shorter adults. They understood nuances, humor, irony, etc., but third, fourth, fifth, and sixth graders were a whole different ball game.

I felt like I had a great relationship with my own kids, and that continues today, even into their adulthood. I thought about how that happened. How did we forge that bond? What I realized was that when they were that age, we usually talked about (because, yes, we were a family of geeks), cartoons, movies, TV shows, comic books, and especially the superhero characters contained therein. So, when I tried it as an icebreaker with my counselees, I was amazed to find that it worked! It facilitated conversations, fostered trust, and promoted sharing. When I wanted to introduce concepts of good character to my students, I went to my go-to subject—superheroes. It worked like the proverbial charm. Not only did they pay attention to me; they couldn't wait for our next session.

Even though I was reluctant to question success, I was still curious as to why the subject of superheroes resonated with my students. Apparently, I am not the only one. Many psychologists have pondered the question in books such as Ben Saunders's *Do the Gods Wear Capes?* (Saunders, 2011). Unfortunately, no one can agree on the exact reason. Some believe that it is because comic books/cartoons are the modern mythology. Writer Ben Shapiro feels that it is not just because it is part of popular culture but because our society needs them.

> "Why do we need superheroes in the first place? Why, in this age of cynicism, do we look to escape to the world of Thor? The answer lies in our dual needs for clarity and hope." (Shapiro, 2011)

Shapiro believes that mythology was created by man to make sense of a confusing world, providing explanations, meaning, logic, and clarity. Furthermore, if the origins of the world are clear and follow logic (as opposed to chaos and chance), then there is hope. Comic book heroes are just our modern versions of mythology.

Writer Eliza Clark believes that our children's fascination with superheroes has to do with changing and gaining power.

> "Each day, as they grow, our kids are discovering their own powers. Their bodies can do more and more, and likewise their minds. In comparison to the babies they used to be, preschoolers really do have superpowers. Once they were helpless babes, but now they can run, jump, and climb! And yet, young children are also keenly aware of their own relative powerlessness. And in some cases, they are also learning that their parents' powers are limited

> too: we can do a lot, but we can't make everything better all the time.
>
> In this developmental context, it's little wonder that superheroes exert such an imaginative pull. The notion of an ordinary, vulnerable person who can transform at will into a hero with superhuman abilities is endlessly appealing to children whose imaginations are far more powerful than their bodies." (Clark, 2012)

In my pursuit of an answer to this question, I even went to the source. I asked Marvel Comics Vice President of Publishing/Executive Editor Tom Brevoort why he thought that kids were obsessed with superheroes. He echoed the sentiments of Clark:

> On the most basic level, being a kid means being largely powerless, and at the mercy of people and institutions that are larger than you—parents, schoolteachers, whomever. A kid has very little control over his life (and for good reason, not that they necessarily see it that way at the time). So a fantasy figure that is larger and stronger and better than all of the teachers and bullies and parents in the world can be a compelling thing. On top of that, there's the appeal of the secret identity, the secret life that nobody else knows about. Also, kids have an innate sense of justice as a black-and-white institution, and so they gravitate towards figures that reinforce or reflect those core beliefs—there's a comforting appeal to them. Plus, bright primary colors and pyrotechnics, what kid doesn't love those?
>
> They are very open to imagination and stimulation and so forth. And so these are all characters and elements that appeal to them. They may not get the shadings and all the aspects of Peter Parker and his powers—his uncle is killed, and he deals with this sense of guilt and responsibility—but they certainly understand he's the guy in red and blue [and] swings around the city doing crazy things and striking poses.

> It's very easy to kind of imagine yourself into the figure. Spider-Man® is one of those characters, and part of that design is so brilliant and beautiful and pure, no matter whom you are—because he's covered head to toe—you can kind of project yourself into that character.

While I had him at my disposal, I also asked Tom if he thought that the good guy should always win.

> I think that the good guys should ultimately always win, but that could be over a very long period of time, and those wins quite often will not be without cost. Some of that is just the nature of storytelling: if you know that the good guy is going to win, it's difficult to sustain either drama or interest. The question, always, is how, and at what cost. This is one of the reasons why Spider-Man became such a popular character—he can triumph over the Vulture or Electro in his superhero identity, but can still go home to a sick aunt or money woes or girl troubles as Peter Parker, troubles that were no doubt accentuated by Peter's need to put on his webbed outfit and take to the skies.

Finally, I asked Tom if there was a feeling in the comic industry that they were obligated to teach a lesson or convey a moral to young people.

> I'm not necessarily convinced that there is an obligation there per se, while it is something that may happen all on its own thanks to the idiom through which we tell our stories. But we don't typically begin with a moral and work backwards from there. Rather, whatever moral there is to observe comes out of the choices the characters make and the results of those choices. There is a strong morality in the Marvel characters, as befits their standing as heroic fiction. But obligation feels too concrete to me. We're bound to tell the best stories we can, guided by our own sense of what is appropriate and whatever the organization's rules may be governing what is and is

> not considered appropriate to publish at each of our ratings levels.

It's good to know that the publishers of comic books understand the weight of responsibility that they possess. In an article written by Joshua Ostroff for Huffington Post, Marvel Editor-In-Chief Axel Alonso agreed with the sentiments of Brevoort but went further: "While parents (ideally) should be role models for life, superheroes remind a child of the moral compass necessary to navigate a universe fraught with thrills and danger." (Ostroff, 2014).

To sum it up, comic books may just be the Grimms' Fairy Tales for the modern generation. The protagonists are people we can identify with, but fantastic things happen to them. In fairy tales and folklore, the supernatural events are attributed to magic. In the comics, these events can generally be explained by the concepts of our scientific understanding: an experiment that goes terribly wrong, exposure to nuclear radiation, a genetic mutation. Whether it's fairy tale or comic book, there is always a moral to the story. Perhaps comics are even an improvement on fairytales in that if you've ever heard the stories of Red Riding Hood and Hansel and Gretel, fairy tales can get pretty vicious and sadistic!

In my original comic book counseling program, I identified the most important aspects of good character and found a comic book superhero that exemplified the essence of each of those character traits. Every two weeks of school, I would present a different PowerPoint presentation to my students. In the original version, I used very recognizable characters from the major comic book publishers, but you might not feel comfortable using copyrighted characters, even in your own classroom.

That is one of the reasons why I created *The Essentialz.* They are my original characters, so I don't need anyone's permission to use them in my counseling program or in a curriculum guide such as this publication. Furthermore, if you are buying this book, then I am giving you expressed permission to use them in your school practice as well.

Also, instead of tweaking a famous comic book character to force-fit the topic that I am trying to teach, each one of the Essentialz characters was specifically designed from the ground up to exemplify an important trait that I want to stress with my students.

Much like my original slide show, the Essentialz slide show that I use in this curriculum explains the backstory of each one of the Essentialz, the character trait he or she exemplifies, and how it might relate to students' own lives.

In between the biweekly presentations, I provide teachers with 'teachable moment' suggestions for weaving the character education concepts into the daily school curriculum. You can find these ideas and suggestions in the beginning part of the following chapters under "Possible Optional Discussion Topics."

Just to raise the excitement level among my students and to hype the importance of the program, I designed t-shirts that looked like the costumes of my heroes or the logos of their teams (the Diggers, Surfers, Gliders, and Bunsens each have their own symbol). I ask the students to guess who we were going to talk about this session and would then reveal the logo under my dress shirt (much like a fictional reporter alter ego for a bigger element of surprise).

4

The Essentialz

LENGTH OF LESSON

30 to 35 minutes

LEARNING OBJECTIVES

- Counselor will introduce the characters that will be discussed in future lessons.
- Students will identify and discuss subject areas that interest them and why.
- Students will recognize that we often have a public persona and a private persona (you can use the terms ‘public and private face’ with your younger students if you like) and how they present themselves to the rest of the world.

KEY CONCEPTS

- Our personal interests contribute to our personality and who we are.
- Impression management is the “me” that we show the world. We can choose to have an honest, transparent one or one that is carefully crafted so that others have a particular opinion of us.

MATERIALS NEEDED

Construction paper, art supplies (e.g., paint)

POSSIBLE OPTIONAL DISCUSSION TOPICS

Being comfortable with your own identity.

ACTIVITY

- On a piece of construction paper, draw two masks.
- On the first mask, depict how you think the world perceives you: bookworm, jock, geek, popular, etc.
- On the second mask, draw a representation of who you really are.
- Discuss the difference between the two masks.

BACKGROUND

In case my students have never read my fiction book, I typically kick off the presentation series with an overview of *The Essentialz.*

The intent is for our students to identify with the Essentialz because the characters are just a little bit older than them, and are what they aspire to be in the near future-their “ego-ideals,” to put it in archaic, Freudian terms (Freud, 1914). The Essentialz also suffer from the same worries, anxieties, and insecurities that our kids do. Although they exemplify good character, the Essentialz are far from perfect. Sometimes they come to a critical moral choice after making a few bad choices, mistakes, or after much soul-searching. They talk like our kids, and they have the same interests and tastes, which nowadays are surprisingly varied and eclectic.

The Essentialz backstory begins with three teens interested in earth sciences (geology, paleontology, etc.) who share the hobby of cave exploring. While in Nevada, they wander into a cave that is so extensive, it borders on the edge of an abandoned test range of the legendary, mysterious Area 51. They discover a strange, glowing, orange rock that erupts in front of them. The explosion shocks them and renders them unconscious. Eventually they come to, and they discover that they are trapped by a cave-in. In their efforts to escape the cave and dig themselves out, they discover that they have superhuman powers.

The three members of this group are Rockie, Maker, and Arsenal.

Rockie. Rockie's real name is Rockwell Norris. He has super strength and can adjust his body density to match any solid on earth–from sand, to rock, to titanium. Rockie is a big guy, but he is gentle and loyal. He is very proud of his Native American heritage.

Maker. Maker's real name is Angela Anning. She is like a human mini-factory or 3-D printer. She can rapidly construct just about anything her team needs (tools, technology, even shelters) from the solids around her. If those solids are large, heavy, or bulky, it's no problem for Angela because, as Maker, she has telekinesis. She lifts them with the power of her mind. Maker is very proud of the quality of her work, but she is socially awkward and more of a follower than a leader.

Arsenal. His real name is Marco Paynes. He is an expert in martial arts. He can create powerful, energy-charged projectiles from any object around him (even dirt). Marco is part African American but is of French heritage. In fact, he is a direct descendant of the French founder of the Knights Templar. Because of this, Arsenal is motivated by a sense of duty and living by a code of honor.

Since all three members develop powers associated with solids, they are represented by the Earth. After their encounter with the strange rock, all three members also discovered the ability to travel quickly via digging subterranean tunnels with remarkable speed. Thus, their nickname is the Diggers.

Three other teen friends are interested in ocean sciences and bond over their love of water sports. While diving off the coast of Florida, they discover a sunken wreck in the Gulf of Mexico and decide to explore it. In the wreck, they encounter a strange, glowing blue object inside a wooden chest (perhaps a sea creature?) The strange object emits bright light that passes through them and renders them unconscious. After the encounter, these teens also find that they are imbued with amazing powers. These three teens are Hydro, Fisk, and Triton.

Hydro. Hydro's real name is Hudson Ballard. He is a fantastically acrobatic surfer. As Hydro, he can assume the form of liquid. Therefore, he can get in anywhere liquids can, which comes in pretty handy. He can also make his body invisible, like clear water. Finally, he can control the surface tension of liquids, so he can 'surf' anywhere using available liquids. Hydro is often the moral compass of his group because he hates lying. However, symbolically, he strives to be as pure and transparent as the liquids he mimics.

Fisk. Fisk's real name is Lark Dhanial Fiske. She can transform into any sea life of any size, from whale to plankton. She is most dangerous when she is a shark or octopus. Fisk's family is from Afghanistan, and they are Muslim. Fisk strives to be a typical American girl, so it really hurts her when strangers jump to the irrational conclusion that she could be a radical Islamist. Fisk is also wheelchair bound, so she fights prejudice on two fronts: her heritage and her disability.

Triton. Triton's real name is Connor Chang. He is of Asian American descent and an expert sailor. He enjoys every kind of water craft from Jet Skis to America's Cup yachts. As Triton, he can command any sea creature to help him, and he can also create massive tidal waves. When he was just discovering how to control his powers, he battled a villain and caused a lot of collateral damage with a rogue wave. Because he (falsely) believed he was responsible for a death, Triton is obsessed with doing enough good to redeem himself.

All of the teens in this group have powers that are connected to water, and all of them can travel quickly via water, above or below the surface. Because of this, their nickname is the Surfers.

Yet another group of teens share a love of daring hobbies enjoyed in the sky. While skydiving over New Jersey, they see a strange, glowing, V-shaped aircraft coming right at them. When it gets close enough to them, they sense that the craft is futuristic because it doesn't look like anything they've ever seen on military websites or in their Civil Air Patrol studies. A strange blue beam emerges from the craft and momentarily stuns them. When the craft disappears, they find they suddenly have special powers, and they need the new powers immediately to prevent them from crashing into Earth. These teens are The Eagle, Turbine, and DM.

The Eagle. The Eagle's real name is Flynn Yeager. Someday he hopes to be a military test pilot. Flynn is called "The Eagle" for several reasons: he can fly, he has enhanced, long-range sight, like an eagle, and he is very patriotic about America. The Eagle can also influence any winged creature do his bidding.

Turbine. Turbine's real name is Gabrielle Geller. Gabby has mental health issues—anxiety, paranoia, and fear. To combat these issues, Gabby forces herself to do audacious daredevil stunts. That is why she is the best skydiver of the group. It's ironic that that Gabby has to fight the instinct to run when faced with danger because as Turbine, she is super-fast and could run away from danger if she wanted to. She can run and spin so quickly, she can even become a human tornado herself!

DM. DM stands for Dark Matter, and her real name is Sarah Sagan. As a teen fascinated with astrophysics, she hopes someday to work for NASA. She thinks that by joining the Civil Air Patrol, she will have good head start. As DM, she can summon any cosmic material like dark matter or nuclear material and use it as a tool or a weapon. Since she can manipulate radioactive isotopes, she can destroy whole worlds with her power, so she has to be extremely responsible with her abilities.

These three teens have powers related to the sky or space. Since they can all travel by air, their nickname is the Gliders.

Our final group is composed of three North Dakota teens who are obsessed with science and experimenting with forms of energy. Just for fun, they try to replicate a Tesla coil and improve upon its performance by using unorthodox materials in the construction. While conducting an experiment with the coil, they see what appears to be a humanoid form in the middle of the plasma field. When they try to get a closer look, they are electrocuted. When they wake up, they discover that they are infused with amazing powers. This group includes Sparks, Fuega, and Tempus.

Sparks. Sparks' real name is Blaise Rogers. Blaise is unique in that he likes learning about both psychology and physics. One of his heroes is the physicist, Nikola Tesla. As Sparks, he commands electricity. He can turn on machines and motors, but can also use lightning bolts as a weapon. However, as a result of his new powers, he also has enhanced synaptic control (the brain runs on electricity, after all) so he has genius-level intelligence. Consequently, he is literally the brains of his group.

Fuega. The alter ego of Fuega, Kiara Edison, is a brilliant mathematician of African American heritage. Fuega can control fire and smoke. It is very apt that she has the powers that she does because fiery describes her to a T. As a result of events early in her life, Kiara has major anger management issues.

Tempus. Tempus's real name is Max Marconi. He can manipulate time and can travel in time as long as it is during the span of his lifetime. Max's father is a wealthy electronics entrepreneur. Max used to act like a rich brat, but traveling through time, he has seen the horrors of famine and world war. As a result, he became much more serious and learned to care for all life.

All members of this group have powers associated with energy and thus represent Fire. They can transform into pure energy and reappear anywhere on Earth, via electrical conduction. Being associated with fire and science, their nickname is the Bunsens.

Originally, the Diggers, Surfers, Gliders, and Bunsens were unaware of each other's existence. Then, when they did all meet, it was almost hatred at first sight. It wasn't until a humanoid named Argo revealed himself to the twelve teens that they stopped their feuding. He tells them that he is from a different dimension called the Zetaverse and that he is responsible for giving them their newfound powers. He did so because he has taken a liking to Earth humans and wants them to avoid the fate of his own species.

He warned them that he could take away their gifts if they do not learn how to get along and act as a team. They will have to do so not only to survive, but also to protect the entire Earth from impending threats. So, the Essentialz added the "z" to their team name in homage to the people of the Zetaverse and to remind them not to suffer their same fate.

The adventures that the Essentialz have from then on involve the following: themes of personality conflicts versus teamwork for the greater good, temptations of power versus responsibility, what it means to be a real hero, and—most of all—crises of conscience.

Each one of the Essentialz has an intriguing backstory, compelling personality trait or quirk, and an inner demon or private challenge they must conquer that should be very familiar to our students.

It is important to note that each one of the twelve characters looks like an ordinary teen when they are not "on the clock". As the stories develop, and as they grow into their powers, they cultivate alter egos, super-personas, and eventually sport team uniforms. I did this specifically to open up the potential for a dialogue with our students on the difference between their public personas and private ones.

As a psychologist, I consider myself a scientist, and I want my students to develop a curiosity about (and hopefully a love of) science. So I like to point out to them that most of my characters share a last name with a famous scientist. Others share a surname with a great American pioneer that I admire, such as X-1 pilot Chuck Yeager, or four-time America's Cup champion Dennis Conner.

During the first week, as an introduction to the characters, I give my students the backstory of the Essentialz.

> *Refer back to the accompanying slide show presentation associated with this chapter.*

DISCUSSION

- Besides extreme sports, most of the Essentialz love one of the disciplines of science (physics, biology, geology, etc.). Is there a subject in school or a hobby that you love? Is there one in which you think you excel?
- The Essentialz don't want fame or fortune (and the dangers associated with that life). Sometimes, they just want to be average teens. So, they have to protect their identities. They try their hardest to keep their 'hero lives' separate from their regular lives. Do you think there is a difference between your 'public persona' (your personality traits that you show to the rest of the world) and your private one?

5

Rockie and Loyalty

LENGTH OF LESSON

30 to 35 minutes

LEARNING OBJECTIVES

- Students will recognize the value of loyalty to individuals, groups, and institutions.
- Students will be able to understand how gangs use loyalty to pressure teens into protecting and advancing their criminal activities.

KEY CONCEPTS

- Membership in a group gives us a sense of belonging, promotes pride and self-confidence.
- Loyalty is an important character trait that helps us maintain friendships and teams, however, it is important to pledge loyalty only to individuals or groups that deserve it.

MATERIALS NEEDED

Art supplies, such as construction paper, crayons, colored pencils, etc.

POSSIBLE OPTIONAL DISCUSSION TOPICS

Discuss how having good manners makes Rockie a more likeable person and why manners are important. Is it okay that some of our world leaders say rude things in their speeches and post unkind things on social media?

ACTIVITY

- Using art supplies, each student will create a flag that portrays their culture, lineage, or even a sports team that they identify with.
- Discuss in class what you put on your flag.
- Why are the things on your flag deserving of your loyalty?
- Break into groups, and discuss how you feel when someone you thought was your friend betrays a confidence.
- Discuss the idea of reciprocity. If you expect loyalty from your friends, what should you give in return?

BACKGROUND

After getting them up to speed with the Essentialz synopsis in the first week, the next time we meet, I provide an overview of the Diggers. For the next three weeks, I take a different Digger and discuss him or her individually.

I generally start with Rockie because he is such a lovable character. Rockwell Norris is a big, quiet, easygoing soul. He is part Shoshone Indian and is very proud of his heritage. In fact, he hopes to be a cultural anthropologist someday. Rockwell often reads about American Indian history, and he believes that his people were exploited and betrayed. Because of this, Rockwell's hot button is loyalty.

He is extremely loyal to his friends Arsenal and Maker. Eventually, when all twelve teens become a team, he is loyal to all of the Essentialz. Because of his politeness and plain-spoken manner, his teammates reciprocate with their loyalty.

When he transforms into Rockie, his body can take on the consistency and density of various types of rock. That's why his face looks like an Easter Island statue. He also doubles in size and acquires super-human strength.

Just for fun, I chose the last name of Norris for Rockie's character as homage to one of my martial arts heroes, Chuck Norris, who is part Cherokee.

The character trait I focus on with Rockie is loyalty. Initially, Rockie resonates with kids because he is so strong and powerful—something that they wish to be. Hopefully, once they get to know him, they will admire him more as a role model of politeness and fidelity.

Our kids give a great deal of lip service to loyalty. They declare to us that they are loyal to their friends with the terms "BFFs" and "squad goals." However, are they truly devoted to the right people or ideals?

We don't have to teach our kids so much about the concept of loyalty as much as we need to teach them to be careful and selective about to whom or to what they are loyal. The main message is whatever it is with which you align yourself, make sure that it is something worthy of your loyalty.

Refer back to the accompanying slide show presentation associated with this chapter.

DISCUSSION

- Do you value loyalty in a friend?
- How do you feel when you think a friend has betrayed a confidence?
- Do your friends think that you are loyal? Can they count on you?
- Rockie believes that being polite is important. Why is that?
- How mannerly are you?

6

Arsenal and Living by a Code of Honor

LENGTH OF LESSON

30 to 35 minutes

LEARNING OBJECTIVES

- Students will recognize the value of personal honor and integrity.
- Students will be able to create their own code of conduct.

KEY CONCEPTS

We all have many people telling us what to do and what is right and wrong: parents, teachers, clergy, and civil authorities. Some of the concepts that we get from these sources we accept and some we may even reject. The ones we accept and keep become our own personal code of conduct.

MATERIALS NEEDED

Poster board, art supplies

POSSIBLE OPTIONAL DISCUSSION TOPICS

Discuss how fighting for your rights compares with being selfish. Many celebrities, billionaire businessmen, and even politicians seem to be concerned with taking care of themselves first instead of helping other people.

ACTIVITY

- Using art supplies, each student will create a knight's shield with a coat of arms of their own design. The coat of arms will have at least three sections that visually depict three rules of their own personal code of honor.
- You can include a motto on your shield such as, "Protect the Helpless."
- Each student will present to the rest of the group their shield and discuss their code.

BACKGROUND

Arsenal is Marco Payne. Marco may seem like he takes himself too seriously sometimes, but it is because he wrestles with internal conflicts. Marco might seem like Hamlet sometimes with his dark and brooding temperament, but it is because he vacillated between a desire for revenge and a sense of honor.

Marco's parents were geologists, and they fostered his love of the science. Unfortunately, while on a science exploration to discover tectonic plates along the Ivory Coast, his parents were killed by a radical African militia group (which happened to be Islamic) seeking to fund their political revolution in a real blood diamond conflict.

Marco's mother was African American, but his father was French. Marco is a direct descendant of Sir Hugues de Payens, the French founder of the Knights Templar. Marco is very proud of this fact and studies the history of the ancient order. The conflict that rages inside Marco is his desire to avenge his parents' deaths versus his desire to live a life of personal integrity and honor.

Arsenal's gift from the Zetaverse entity, Argo, is the ability to pick up any solid object (even dirt on the ground), charge it with energy, and throw it as a powerful projectile weapon.

One of the concepts I really like to play up in my presentation is the fact that since Marco's family was murdered with a gun, Arsenal detests lethal, bullet-shooting guns. He knows all other martial arts from karate to fencing, but he will never touch a firearm.

In my Arsenal presentation, the nickname that his teammates give him is The Dirt Knight (an obvious homage to a certain moody, dark, comic book dude), and he truly lives his life like a knight.

As a descendant of the Knights Templar, Marco is connected to the precursor of the Freemason Society. The Knights originated during the Crusades to help protect unarmed religious pilgrims in their journeys to worship in the Holy Land of Jerusalem. As a Chevalier (Knight) of this order, one has to pledge their commitment to lifelong acts of charity as well as dedicate oneself to study the history of the Templar Knights.

Arsenal is much like a fighting Christian monk of the thirteenth century because they both live according to a code of honor. Even though Arsenal may be tempted by revenge, he is still a good role model for our students because honor is an important concept of good character. The message is a vital one: personal integrity is an extremely difficult thing to get back once you lose it, so always temper your actions against whether the consequences will maintain or damage your honor.

That being said, one of the points of conflict in the Essentialz' story lines is that Marco's basic instinct is to generalize his anger and hold a grudge against all Muslims because of his parent's death. Sometimes, in his weaker moments, he even takes it out on another member of the Essentialz that is Muslim (we'll talk about Fisk later). Eventually, Marco realizes that a true, honorable knight would not do that. If it were not for his sense of integrity, he might have never conquered his prejudice, and he would have missed out on a great friendship with Fisk.

As a member of the Knights Templar SMOTJ-USA, I often find myself at odds with other organizations that claim to be Templars and promote prejudice against Muslims by calling for a new, modern Crusade. True Templar Knights would never condone such intolerance and violence against anyone.

Again, I will say that our children are watching us. I am concerned that there are certain adults out there that may hold sway over our students that are more interested in building walls to keep out foreigners than finding ways to bridge our differences.

In this slide show, I enumerate the true Templar Knights' Code, because I am familiar with it in my own life, and because it is a pretty good one. However, one activity that you can do with your students in order to help them have a personal connection with this lesson is to have them create their own code of honor. Most knights carry a shield into battle, so you can even have them create their own shields with their own honor-themed family crest and corresponding motto.

Refer back to the accompanying slide show presentation associated with this chapter.

DISCUSSION

This is the Templar Knight's Code of Honor:

- Protect the weak
- Be kind to others
- Be polite
- Be trustworthy
- Be honest
- NEVER turn your back on someone in trouble, even if they are your enemy!

7

Maker and Being a Good Team Member

LENGTH OF LESSON

30 to 35 minutes

LEARNING OBJECTIVES

- Students will recognize the value of being a good team member.
- Students will be able to recognize the value in compromise.

KEY CONCEPTS

- We can't all be leaders all the time. That might not be very productive. The way societies are successful, and how the world as a whole functions is when some of us say, "okay, let's try it your way."
- Throughout your school career, instructors will expect you to participate in group projects and presentations. Those groups

that have members that know their roles and do their fair share are the ones that succeed.

MATERIALS NEEDED

Paper or plastic cups, rubber bands and string

POSSIBLE OPTIONAL DISCUSSION TOPICS

Angela is socially awkward. Are you always comfortable in social situations?

ACTIVITY—PLASTIC CUP STACKING CHALLENGE GAME INSTRUCTIONS

- Teacher prep: using the materials above, tie four or five strings to a rubber band. Make as many of these grabbers as there are groups in your class. Students will break up into groups of five or six.
- Each group will assign a leader. The other members must grab a string and pick up cups using only the rubber band part of their grabbers. They are to make a tower of cups using only their grabbers to build it (no hands!) The leader's job is to give them direction.

BACKGROUND

Maker is a notable character because she is very comfortable not being a leader of the group. That's an important trait to review with our kids. Too often, we obsess over telling our kids to "be a leader." That's not always the best advice. If everyone were the leader, nothing would get done.

Maker is Angela Anning. She is leaning towards becoming a paleontologist because she admits that she sometimes "deals better with dead dinosaurs than living people." I named Angela after famous paleontologist Mary Anning.

While Arsenal is the leader of the Diggers group, that is just fine with Angela. She has idolized Marco as a big brother ever since the day that her family took him in after his parents were murdered.

Maker's Essentialz power is articulated telekinesis over all solids. She can pick up things with her mental powers and mold them into any product she wishes, whether it be a tool or an entire shelter big enough to house all the Essentialz.

Angela struggles with social skills and awkwardness. Strangely enough, sometimes blurting out things instead of being more subtle actually works to her advantage. Even if she cringes at her own social ineptitude, she is still very proud of her powers and the quality of her workmanship when she makes things.

There are many instances in the comic books where the superheroes' awesome sidekicks are great followers and some that eventually strike out on their own, becoming heroes in their own right—not that Maker would ever do that—but she is very capable of it. Even though she is more comfortable with others being the lead dogs, she is more than just a sidekick. She can be fierce and heroic when she needs to be.

Reviewing the story of Maker is a great way to introduce to our kids the topics of shyness, mastering social skills, and being able to follow direction at school. I often follow it up with the Cup-Stacking Challenge game to highlight the importance of following directions from a leader.

> *Refer back to the accompanying slide show presentation associated with this chapter.*

DISCUSSION

- What would probably happen if we all were the leaders and no one wanted to follow anyone else's directions?
- When a group of six people want to decide on a restaurant for dinner, and two want Mexican food, two want Chinese, and the last two want Italian, what should they do?
- Sometimes it's OK to be a follower instead of a leader—as long as your leader is a good one!
- Being a good student not only means being open to learning, but also being open to—and able to—follow directions.

8

Hydro and Honesty

LENGTH OF LESSON

30 to 35 minutes

LEARNING OBJECTIVES

- Students will recognize the value of honesty.
- Students will be able to recognize the difference between sharing facts and offering an opinion. Many times our students think they are just being 'brutally honest' but what they are really doing is just being intentionally hurtful.

KEY CONCEPTS

- One of the best ways to obtain and maintain friends is to have a reputation for honesty.
- Again, reciprocity is important: if you hate that feeling when you find out a friend has lied to you, then you must be a good, honest friend who would not want your bestie to experience that awful feeling.

MATERIALS NEEDED

- For this activity, teachers must bravely volunteer the use of their cell phone with full volume on (using a student's phone is probably not a good option)
- The use of a classroom phone that can make outside calls
- One chair at the front of the room

POSSIBLE OPTIONAL DISCUSSION TOPICS

Hudson is a child of divorce, and he has a stepfather. Can you think of any issues that might come with being part of a blended family?

ACTIVITY—PANTS ON FIRE GAME INSTRUCTIONS

- The players close their eyes and form a circle facing outward. The teacher may ask them to rotate in the circle so no one can memorize positions. The teacher will silently tap one student and give them the cell phone. The student will hide it on themselves. Next, the teacher will tell everyone to open their eyes.
- Each student will have a turn in the "hot seat"—the chair at the front of the room, while the other players ask them questions about having the phone. The one with the hidden phone must lie and say that they do not have it. All players will vote on who is the liar. Finally, the teacher will use the classroom phone to call their cell phone. When the cell rings, the liar will be revealed.
- Close out with a group discussion on the emotions involved in lying.

BACKGROUND

Now that we are done with the Diggers, next we move on to the Essentialz that gain their power from water: The Surfers.

After a quick overview of the Surfers, why they are friends, and how they obtained their powers, I directly move on to Hydro.

Hydro is Hudson Ballard. Although he seems like a hippie-inspired, airhead surfer dude, he is really bright and wants to be an oceanographer. In fact, I named him after famous oceanographer Robert Ballard.

Originally, Hudson was not serious about school. He would often cut school to go surfing.

One day, a hurricane passed near his coastal Florida home. That morning, Hudson lied to his parents, cut school, and went surfing instead to catch the gnarly waves that the storm was supposed to kick up.

Unfortunately, the hurricane deviated from its course and slammed right into the coast. Most people evacuated, but Hudson could not. He found shelter and hunkered down. When the schools evacuated, Hudson's parents panicked when they did not find him with his classmates. Hudson's brother, Mark, volunteered to go out in the storm and find him. When a light pole fell and hit his truck in the height of the storm, Mark died.

Afterwards, Hudson's family crumbled under the weight of their grief. His parents split up. He blames himself not only for his brother's death but for his parent's divorce. He vows never to lie again because of the suffering that it caused.

When Argo studied the human teens, he noted Hudson's pain and gave him the power to transform into Hydro. Hydro's power is the ability to assume a liquid state. Hydro is very talented at surveillance and evading security because he can get in anywhere liquids can. He can even make himself transparent just like water. Hudson likes this because he feels like he can make himself look as pure as he wished he was.

When his parents split up, they struggled financially on their own. Hudson contemplated using his powers to steal from banks and stores to help his family, but his father told him that he needed to be a force for good.

Since Hudson vowed never to lie again, he shared the secret of Hydro with his dad and stepdad. It was the right decision. His dad told him, "Life isn't easy for anybody, whether you're normal or exceptional, but you got your powers for a reason."

The character trait that I focus on with Hydro is honesty. Honesty needs to be important to our school-age kids; not only to prevent plagiarism and cheating on tests, but also to counter the fact that many adults they encounter today seemingly don't hold integrity in high regard. Another sidebar discussion opportunity in this lesson, especially if you teach social studies to older students, could be discussions about truth in advertising, or taking credit for someone else's work.

Hudson's story is also a good opportunity to open a dialogue with our kids about divorce, adoption, and blended families.

Refer back to the accompanying slide show presentation associated with this chapter.

DISCUSSION

- Is the truth important to you?
- Do you value honesty in a friend?
- How do you feel when someone lies to you?
- Hydro was taught to be a good person by his family. Do you believe that you are just born a certain way or can you change?

9

Triton and Forgiveness

LENGTH OF LESSON

30 to 35 minutes

LEARNING OBJECTIVES

- Students will recognize the value of forgiveness, which leads to healing.
- Students will be able to understand that sometimes holding a grudge can destroy friendships that deserve saving.
- Students will learn about restorative justice, where the harm is repaired and the relationship with friends or the community as a whole is restored.

KEY CONCEPTS

Everyone makes mistakes. It's what we learn from these mistakes that matters. Can we learn to forgive others who have hurt us? What can we do to earn trust back from the people that we have wronged? Does everyone deserve a second chance?

MATERIALS NEEDED

Paper, pens, small bucket of water

POSSIBLE OPTIONAL DISCUSSION TOPICS

Comic books and movies are full of stories where villains turn over a new leaf and become heroes. Is that realistic?

ACTIVITY

Making a mistake in a relationship, gossiping, and hurting others with words or actions not only harms the victim but also creates a heavy burden for the offender to carry around. One way to start the feeling is to forgive oneself and lighten the burden.

- On some paper, write down a time where you let down your friends or family, or something that you did to hurt someone, or even something that you are not proud of.
- When you are done writing, rip up the paper and throw the pieces in a trashcan.
- As you throw it away, imagine that your mistake disappears—this is what it's like to ask for forgiveness.
- Discuss how that makes you feel.

BACKGROUND

Although the potential for themes of forgiveness and redemption are certainly there in the story of Hydro, I usually reserve those topics for when I discuss Triton.

Triton is Connor Chang, an Asian American who is an expert at sailing and piloting watercraft of all kinds. Whether it's stunt trick—riding a Jet Ski or mastering the helm of an America's Cup yacht racer, Connor can captain any vessel, like his namesake, America's Cup famous champion, Dennis Connor.

Before he became one of the Essentialz, Connor could really hold a grudge. Once he lost a sailing race to a friend, and he refused to congratulate him or even talk to him because he believed his friend used dirty tactics to win. Connor refused to forgive him.

When Argo transformed Connor into an Essential, he gave him the power to control the seas. He could make water flow anywhere and create powerful waves. He can also talk to all water-dwelling creatures. Connor adopted the name of Triton, which was the name of one of the sons of the Greek god, Poseidon.

Connor's very proud personality made it very hard for him to forgive anyone, but that all changed. In the Essentialz, when he was just learning to master his powers as Triton, he summoned a tidal wave that was meant for a bad guy. He lost control of the wave and for a while he mistakenly believed that he had drowned an innocent teen due to his actions (later, the other Essentialz proved to him that the teen had died before the wave came).

Connor carried around a lot of guilt because of that accident, and he is always trying to find ways to make amends and undo the damage he believes he has done. A major motivator for Triton's actions is the need for redemption.

Because of this incident, Triton is usually the member of the team that is the most forgiving and the first one that is ready to give an enemy a second chance.

The discussion of Triton is especially important to the development of good character.

Many of our students want to emulate our heroes, but they consistently have been told by adults how bad they are. So often these kids just give up on trying to be good because they have been programmed into believing that they are too far down the wrong path to be saved.

We can correct that. The first way we can do that in this counseling program is by highlighting the fact that all of the Essentialz have human failings, and some have made some pretty awful mistakes. In some cases, our student's transgressions seem almost trivial in comparison. Another, more important way that we can reorient our students is to show them that there are quite a few examples in classic literature and movies of heroes that used to be bad guys.

The Grinch, Ebenezer Scrooge, and Darth Vader are but a few examples of villains that turned over a new leaf or sought redemption by the end of their stories. Jean Valjean in Victor Hugo's *Les Miserables* (Hugo, 1862) is another example of a character that committed crimes in the beginning of the story in order to survive but became the most admirable, beloved protagonist by the end. The comic books are chock full of even more examples of villains who changed their ways to become heroes.

This could not have happened for these characters if they did not desire redemption. It also could not have happened without established heroes showing them compassion and forgiveness.

Our lesson for this session is twofold: one is to show those students that are down on themselves for their behaviors that it's not too late to turn it around. They should not brand themselves as "lost causes." There are many ways to make up for their behavior, so that they are welcomed back to the school community unconditionally. This is a great opportunity to open a frank discussion with students about the concept of restorative justice—where offenders meet with their victims and ask for forgiveness.

Our second aim of this lesson is to show other students the virtue of forgiveness and compassion. Ask them how they feel when someone refuses to forgive them. Everyone messes up now and then. While it is true that we want our students to make life decisions as if there were no reset button, we also want to teach them that the majority of human beings need and often deserve a second chance.

Again, this is a tightrope that we ask our kids to walk. We want them to be safe, smart, and not allow themselves to be victimized. But at the same time, it is an important lesson that when we hold a grudge unnecessarily, we may lose a valuable ally.

Refer back to the accompanying slide show presentation associated with this chapter.

DISCUSSION

- Everyone can find redemption if they are really serious about it.
- If you are on the wrong path, it is NEVER too late to turn around and start down the right road.
- NO ONE is perfect.
- Everyone needs forgiveness now and then.
- How do YOU feel when you've done something wrong and the other person refuses to forgive you?
- Do you believe that everyone has the potential for good?

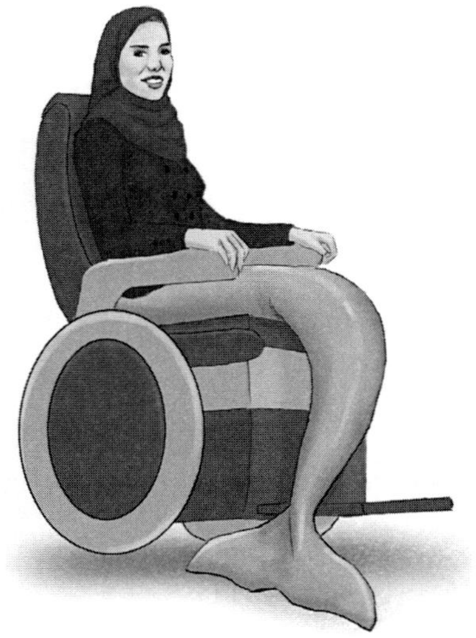

10

Fisk, Overcoming Disabilities and Discrimination

LENGTH OF LESSON

35 to 40 minutes

LEARNING OBJECTIVES

- Students will recognize the unfairness of discrimination and how to confront and combat prejudice.
- Students will recognize several forms of discrimination, such as discrimination based on race, gender, religion, and sexual orientation.
- Students will also recognize that people who are differently-abled can be discriminated against as well.
- Students will understand the definitions of diversity and tolerance.

KEY CONCEPTS

- Being judged on our character simply by the way we look, worship, or love is wrong. Much like bullying, we don't want it to happen to us, so we cannot sit by idly if we see it happening to others.
- As a society, we are moving away from identifying people as disabled because of its negative connotation and we are recognizing their situation as differently-abled. Often, these people rely more on what they can do to make up for what they are unable to do.

MATERIALS NEEDED

Teachers may choose to go high-tech or low-tech in this activity. If they have a connected classroom, they can use an online polling app, or, if you prefer the nonelectronic way, small pieces of notepaper of the same color and pencils are all you need.

POSSIBLE OPTIONAL DISCUSSION TOPICS

Being able to morph into a fish not only made Fisk feel freer; it also helped her identify with sea creatures and understand their survival instincts. This is a quality known as 'empathy'. How does empathy help to combat prejudice?

ACTIVITY—RED VS. BLUE GAME INSTRUCTIONS

- Being discriminated against produces a lot of powerful emotions. If people were more aware of the emotional toll that prejudice took on its victims, perhaps they would be more aware of the harm that they were doing and less inclined to acting that way.
- In this activity, the counselor announces that the class is being broken up into two groups: The Reds and the Blues. After dividing the class, the counselor announces that the Reds are overall better, so he/she is going to reward them with homework passes (no homework). After a minute or two to let that sink in, the counselor announces that he or she has made a mistake, and the Blues are better and going to get the homework passes instead.
- After the counselor announces that this was just an experiment, he or she asks the students (via the online poll or by writing it on notepaper) how they felt being part of the privileged group

and how they felt when they were part of the disadvantaged group. Discuss the results.

BACKGROUND

Fisk is one of the most intriguing of the Essentialz—so much so that her story opens up dialogue for several discussions. You can break them up into two sessions or combine them together into one.

Fisk is Lark Dhaniel Fiske. She is a paraplegic. Typically, this could present as an impediment to her preferred choice of study (she wants to be a marine biologist). Fortunately, though, Lark is no ordinary girl with an ordinary drive to succeed, and her father is no ordinary man. As a brilliant engineer, he has designed some amazing pieces of technology that allow Lark to be mobile on land (a smart wheelchair) and study ocean life (mechanical fins).

When Argo turned her into one of the Essentialz, Lark shortened her last name from Fiske to Fisk, the Norwegian word for fish. This is appropriate because her Essentialz power is the ability to become any form of sea life. She can become as tiny and unobtrusive as plankton or as huge and powerful as a blue whale. Even with her assistive devices, Lark's movement is still limited, but she is completely free and unencumbered when she transforms into Fisk. This has caused internal conflict for her: should she stay a fish and be completely free or tolerate her limitations on land in order to maintain her human relationships?

One of the most important takeaways for this lesson is the importance of attitude. With a negative attitude, it doesn't matter what kind of setback you are dealing with; you are defeated before you even start. With a positive one, people have created the pyramids, the Panama Canal and other wonders of the world. The notion of your attitude determining how much you will achieve is often a concept that successful motivational coaches like to use.

On the one hand, the story of Fisk allows us to discuss with our students the following: overcoming our limitations, using our strengths to marginalize our weaknesses, how attitude can impact results, and starting a conversation about being fair (but not condescending) to those that are differently abled.

On the other hand, Lark Dhaniel Fiske deals with not only a disability but also several levels of prejudice. You see, besides being differently abled, Lark is also an Afghan American and a Muslim.

She desperately wants to just be a typical American girl that happens to be of the Islamic faith, but she often has to endure religious intolerance and profiling. She has earned the respect and friendship of her Essentialz teammates but not before there were harsh words and hard feelings in the beginning.

An additional topic that you can cover with your students still uses Fisk, but addresses the topics of diversity and tolerance.

One of the most commonsense notions of good character is fairness for everyone. The concepts of diversity, tolerance, and justice are distinct, but they all connect back to fairness, which is one of the Six Pillars of Character, according to www.charactercounts.org.

To clarify, diversity studies relate to the understanding that everyone is unique and that we should recognize our individual differences. These differences can include the following:

- Race
- Ethnicity
- Gender
- Sexual orientation
- Age
- Abilities
- Religious beliefs
- Political beliefs

Diversity education is the exploration of these differences in a safe, positive, and nurturing environment. I recognize that we are different from each other, and I appreciate that and even celebrate the differences that you bring to the world. Diversity means understanding that each individual is unique, and that we recognize our individual differences and can accept and even celebrate them. These differences could be race, ethnicity, gender, age, physical abilities, religious beliefs, or even how much money your family has. No matter who or what you are, you are entitled to live in a safe, positive, respectful, and nurturing environment.

Tolerance is related, but just a bit different. Despite a slightly negative connotation of when you 'merely tolerate' someone, tolerance goes beyond studying differences and acknowledging them to actually accepting them and helping people deal with their differences to function in an open, free society. Tolerance means a fair, objective, and accepting attitude toward those who have opinions, beliefs, practices, racial or ethnic origins, etc., which are different from our own. It means freedom from bigotry.

Justice, then, includes the laws we try to hammer out and enact in order to ensure that everyone is treated equally and the corresponding consequences meted out by peers and governments if someone violates that tolerance. This often requires open discourse, dialogue, a consensus about what is fair, and even compromise. Think of it as a process.

Because we are different, we are not always going to agree, and I accept that and I'm even alright with that. Justice. When we do disagree, let's work out a system of rules for airing our grievances with each other that is fair for everyone, because that's what a civilized society does.

Comic books do a great job with themes of justice. However, they have done a so-so job of addressing the subject of tolerance. What the comic book publishers are really making an effort on lately is racial and cultural diversity in their protagonists. In the 1940s and 1950s, the vast majority of comic book heroes were white men.

As publishers realized that more girls and racial minorities read their books, they added more diverse lead characters to reflect the multiplicity of their audience.

In creating the Essentialz, I took great effort to make sure that half the characters were female, and that African American, Hispanic, American Indian, Asian and Middle Eastern ethnicities were represented.

My PowerPoint slides for this chapter concentrate on overcoming disabilities, and diversity, but this lesson can create an opportunity for a group discussion on tolerance, fairness, and justice, too.

> *Refer back to the accompanying slide show presentation associated with this chapter.*

DISCUSSION

- Heroes are not all Caucasian.
- Heroes come in all shapes, sizes (even as small as a plankton); and racial, ethnic, and religious backgrounds.

- What are you good at?
- What are you not so good at?
- Can you use your areas of strength to make up for your areas of weakness?
- Do you think that you would know discrimination if you saw it?
- Now that you experienced prejudice in our game, what can you do to stop it/prevent it in real life?
- Discuss the concept that that good people need to act to prevent bad people from doing bad things.

11

Turbine and Overcoming Fear

LENGTH OF LESSON

30 to 35 minutes

LEARNING OBJECTIVES

- Students will understand that although fear can be an instinct of self-preservation, it can also be a psychological disability.
- Students will recognize ways in which to confront and conquer fears that are unproductive.

KEY CONCEPTS

Fear was useful when humans were evolving. Sometimes, however, fear can be debilitating. At best, they can get in the way of us doing some exciting things; at worst, it can paralyze us and affect the quality of life. Strategies, friendships, help from others, and even faith can help us cope with fear.

MATERIALS NEEDED

Whiteboard

POSSIBLE OPTIONAL DISCUSSION TOPICS

Even though Turbine can run away from just about anything, she cannot run away from her problems or her fears. Is it a good strategy to run away from ours?

ACTIVITY

- This activity is simple and straightforward. No symbolism is necessary. Students will discuss strategies for coping and dealing with fear. The counselor will write down the best ones on a whiteboard.
- If students have difficulty starting, the counselor can help out with suggestions like controlled breathing, and self-talk.
- Brainstorm ways in which we can cope with scary situations. What is your favorite?

BACKGROUND

We are now on to our next group of teens, the Gliders, who have powers associated with the air or the cosmos.

One of the things that drove me nuts about early comics was the ease in which the heroes nonchalantly jumped into a dangerous situation and fearlessly saved the day—no mention of any trepidation or concerns about self-preservation there at all. It doesn't take a psychologist like me to recognize that's not normal human behavior. That's one of the reasons I created Turbine.

Turbine is Gabrielle Geller (named after a famous scientist Robert Geller, who studied everything from geophysics to tornadoes). Gabby would like to be a meteorologist one day, but she thinks that she could never be the kind that goes on TV because of her anxieties.

One thing that you have to admire about Gabby is that she tries to cope with her fears head-on. She suffers from panic attacks, anxiety, and even paranoid ideations, but she tries to battle those feelings with a self-therapy that is known as "flooding," invented by psychologist Thomas Stampfl (Stampfl, 1967). The best way she knows how to master her fears is to put herself squarely in dangerous situations. That is why she practices extreme sports, like skydiving, with her friends.

As Turbine, she has super speed, even to the point of being able to create tornadoes with her velocity. Due to her anxiety problems, whenever there is danger, her first instinct is to run away—fast; but Turbine fights these urges so she can be a good teammate and help her friends.

The point of her character is that (unlike those stoic and 'fearless' heroes of the 1940s and 1950s comic books) she has the same fears as the rest of us. In fact, they are probably more intense for her than the average person, but she refuses to succumb to them. Instead, she confronts them head on, and that is the way to deal with fear.

One of the things that I loved about my dad was that he taught me this lesson about fear years ago.

There was an amusement park in our area that had a gunfighter arcade game complete with a mechanical cowboy adversary that, I swear, to my 5-year-old eyes seemed every bit of seven feet tall. He resembled Yul Brynner's character in the movie, *Westworld* (Crichton, 1973), and he was dark and menacing. Worst of all, his eyes lit up red when he challenged you to a shootout, and I was scared witless of him. When my dad caught on to my terror as I watched teenage boys lose to him, he walked in front of the game and called me over. He said, "I'm going to put some coins in this game, and we are going to do this together." Three times, with my dad guiding me, I pulled the arcade gun out of the holster, and we beat him to the draw. By the time we were done, I was laughing with glee as the mechanical outlaw groaned. "Ahhh, ya GOT me, pardner!!" Afterwards my dad got down on my level and calmly said, "Face your fears, and they will disappear."

I am proud to say that I used this same method with my own daughter, who cowered in fear of the woods when I suggested a nature hike. With my dad's technique, I showed her that if you let fear govern your life, you will miss out on a lot of fun things.

Because Gabby Geller has some clinical diagnoses, Turbine is a great character for not only addressing fear, but also for discussions about the many forms of mental illness.

Refer back to the accompanying slide show presentation associated with this chapter.

DISCUSSION

- What kinds of fears do you have?
- How do you act when you are afraid?
- Do you think that you can run away from your problems?
- How can you become master of your fears?
- What do we mean when we say, "Face your fears, and they will disappear?"

12

Dark Matter and Responsibility

LENGTH OF LESSON

30 to 35 minutes

LEARNING OBJECTIVES

- Students will understand that responsibility is one of the most important aspects of adulthood.
- Students will recognize the importance of their responsibilities such as homework, chores, taking care of family pets, etc.

KEY CONCEPTS

In civilized society, everyone has a job and everyone has responsibilities. If we do not take care of our responsibilities, we might starve, die of illness, or live in unsanitary conditions. We must all do our part, because others may be depending on us.

MATERIALS NEEDED

Whiteboard, notecards, pencils

POSSIBLE OPTIONAL DISCUSSION TOPICS

Respect goes hand in hand with responsibility.

ACTIVITY

- In this activity, the counselor will write on a whiteboard a statement that sounds like a person making an excuse or shirking responsibility.
- Using the notecards, the students will rewrite the statements so that they sound like someone is taking responsibility. The excuse statements can be sentences like:

  "It's broken."

  "He makes me mad."

  "Everyone else was late, too."

  "I couldn't do it because the directions weren't clear."

BACKGROUND

Although Rockie is very strong, the most powerful of the Essentialz is Dark Matter. DM, as her friends like to call her, is Sarah Sagan (you guessed it: I named her after cosmology superstar Carl Sagan). Sarah is über-responsible. She wants to be a scientist and astronaut for NASA someday, so she studies hard and juggles lots of responsibilities: school, an after-school job, and serving in the Civil Air Patrol because she hopes the experiences will make her an ideal space program candidate.

It's a good thing that Sarah is so responsible because her awesome Essentialz power could prove cataclysmic in the wrong hands. DM has the ability to summon any material found in the cosmos. That includes cosmic energy, dark matter, radioactive material, and even the planet-crushing gravity of a black hole. If she wanted, she could annihilate a continent with a nuclear blast or have a planet sucked into gravitational oblivion.

With such destructive power, DM could let it go to her head. She could abuse it to obliterate her enemies or anyone who stood in her way. Worse yet, she could delude herself into thinking that she is a god, but she does not. Sarah is much too grounded, ethical, and sane to be that careless with her gift.

The main lesson of DM is one of the most important concepts of good character for our kids because it is so basic but so all-encompassing. It even has parallels in the Bible. Jesus told his disciples, "To whom men have committed much, of him they will ask the more." (Luke 12:48 King James Bible Version). To put it in other words (as many other writers have): With power comes coinciding influence.

If you want to drive a car, you'd better know and obey the traffic laws. If you want to own a gun, you'd better know how to handle it safely and respect its deadly capabilities. If you want to have children, you'd better be ready for the responsibilities of being a good parent. If you want to hold an elected office, you'd better not betray the public's trust.

The benefit of self-control is the secondary message of the presentation for DM. Controlling the impulse to hit a peer that is bothering them or to battle the compulsion to take a coveted item that does not belong to them is a valuable lesson for our students, and is not as obvious to them as you may think.

> *Refer back to the accompanying slide show presentation associated with this chapter.*

DISCUSSION

- What does it mean when we say, "To those that are given much, much is required?"
- Everyone has responsibilities at school!
- Do your homework
- Do your best
- Follow the rules
- Be kind, polite, and respectful of others

13

The Eagle and Good Citizenship

LENGTH OF LESSON

30 to 35 minutes

LEARNING OBJECTIVES

- Students will understand the practices of good citizenship.
- Students will recognize their responsibilities in regards to registering to vote, voting on a consistent basis, and understanding and discussing issues without acrimony.

KEY CONCEPTS

- Good citizenship is more than just proclaiming out loud that someone loves his or her country. It also means promoting fairness for everyone, exercising freedom of speech, and not denying other citizens their rights.

- Good citizens pick candidates to represent them based on where they stand on the issues, their record, and related experience, not because of their looks, wealth, or personality.

MATERIALS NEEDED

Construction paper, art supplies

POSSIBLE OPTIONAL DISCUSSION TOPICS

Social studies cross-curriculum topic: What are the qualities of an effective government?

ACTIVITY—THE CAMPAIGN GAME

In this activity, students will imagine that they are running for public office. Using the construction paper, each student will create campaign posters that express his or her platform, and/or he or she will design bumper stickers with their campaign slogan.

A discussion will follow, centering around whether the posters and slogans effectively express good citizenship concepts.

BACKGROUND

The Eagle is one of the characters that is sometimes admirable and sometimes aggravating. He is passionate, especially about his country, but sometimes his passion gets in the way of his reason. When he gets angry, he might lash out without thinking, and he can say some hurtful things.

The Eagle is Flynn Yeager (named after famous test pilot Chuck Yeager). He loves to fly aircraft, and he can't wait to get his hands on a fighter jet when he is old enough to join the military. Until then, he flies anything from crop dusters to helicopters, dreaming of the day that he can be part of the heralded Red Flag Squadron of the Air Force.

The Eagle's power that he obtained from Argo is the ability to summon any avian creature (from a single tiny hummingbird to convocation of eagles) and have it do his bidding. He also has enhanced visual acuity of 20/4, literally giving him eagle eyes.

Flynn is a super-patriot, but sometimes his enthusiasm borders on jingoism. Because of this, he may spout off some opinionated, isolationist, hawkish, and even intolerant ideas before his friends have a chance to set him straight, but eventually they do—especially Fisk.

In fits of frustration, he has spewed some undeserved venom in Fisk's direction. When they first meet, Eagle and Fisk mistrust each other but finally bond as reliable friends. As such, Fisk often has to calm Eagle down or talk some sense into him, but just as often, she is his foil and has to knock him down a few pegs. In the novel, I thought it a valuable lesson to show that a super-patriot white boy and a Muslim American girl could be friends.

In this lesson, it is important to show that even though The Eagle is a hero, he sometimes has flawed ideals. If everyone thought the way he did, we would have many politicians in office who may be very isolationist or prone to influence from special interest groups and not very interested in consensus building, bipartisan compromise, or the greater good. Sadly, we do have politicians like that from time-to-time, but if everyone was as inflexible as Flynn, we would have a whole legislature building full of them.

Hopefully, we can convince our students not to be focused on being right all of the time. They should be more interested in fairness, equal rights for all, and democracy.

Refer back to the accompanying slide show presentation associated with this chapter.

DISCUSSION

Good citizenship includes many facets:

- Loyalty to country.
- Fairness for everyone.
- A dedication to make things better for others.

14

Fuega and Controlling Anger

LENGTH OF LESSON

30 to 35 minutes

LEARNING OBJECTIVES

- Students will understand the natural consequences of anger.
- Students will develop coping mechanisms for dealing with their anger.
- Students will learn to express their anger in socially acceptable ways.

KEY CONCEPTS

- Uncontrolled anger can hurt people and destroy friendships.
- Anger is also unhealthy. Furthermore, there are natural consequences of anger. People avoid angry, bitter people, or they get

angry back at them. If we don't learn how to control anger, we will lead a lonely existence.

MATERIALS NEEDED

3" × 5" inch notecards

POSSIBLE OPTIONAL DISCUSSION TOPICS

Anger can lead to aggression and violence. Have you ever witnessed a fight or even been in one yourself because of anger? How could it have been avoided?

ACTIVITY—I WAS SO MAD GAME INSTRUCTIONS

- Students will sit in a circle. For Round 1, each student will take a turn finishing the sentence, "I was so mad that I…" with a silly thought. If they cannot come up with their own answer, they will pick a card and read the silly answer on it, such as "painted the dog green," or "made a cactus sandwich," or "ate my own homework."
- At the beginning of the second round, the counselor announces that they are going to get a bit more serious, and this time they will finish the sentence, "I was so mad that I…" with something constructive such as "took a walk to calm down," or "painted a picture," or "counted to ten."

BACKGROUND

We are on our last group of teens, the North Dakota friends who are big fans of chemistry, electricity, and physics that I lovingly nicknamed the Bunsens.

The first of this group is Fuega. Her power is the ability to start fires. Unfortunately, this power is connected to Fuega's mood. When under control, she can start little fires. When she really gets mad, though, she causes a firestorm that even she has difficulty controlling.

Fuega is the alter ego of Kiara Fernandez Edison, a girl of mixed ethnicity. She is African American and Hispanic (and yes, her namesake is inventor Thomas Edison). Kiara is a brilliant mathematician that is interested in physics. Because of her mixed race and her nerdiness, she has had to endure bullying. Before she was transformed into Fuega by Argo, she was quiet, but intense anger always seethed just underneath the surface of her persona.

Fuega's gift of fire starting is a double-edged sword: it can be helpful to her team, but it can rage out of control and do unintended damage. This is why Kiara has to struggle to keep her emotions in check. She cannot be harmed by her own fire, but she can hurt others, including her friends.

Kiara is an excellent vehicle for discussing anger management with students. I often touch upon how anger (whether it is outright violent acts or hurtful words) can hurt others. Additionally, I like to point out to them that having a bad temper makes it hard to keep friends.

An even bigger-picture concept that Fuega opens up for discussion is that self-control is a pretty good idea in many areas of life: nutrition, watching TV, etc.

Discuss with your student how to use a coping strategy:

- Express your anger in nondestructive ways.
- Count to 10 or 20.
- Calmly tell someone that you are angry—say—don't show your anger.
- Use 'replacement words' instead of foul language or hurtful words.
- Write your feelings in a journal.
- Exercise—release endorphins!
- Always remind yourself: words and actions are like toothpaste: Once they are out, you can't get them back!

Refer back to the accompanying slide show presentation associated with this chapter.

DISCUSSION

- Can you recognize when you are angry?
- Did you think you could hurt others (with words or actions) when you are angry?
- How do you deal with your anger?
- What works? What doesn't?

15

Tempus and Caring (and Respect)

LENGTH OF LESSON

30 to 35 minutes

LEARNING OBJECTIVES

- Students will understand the benefits of caring, including greater self-esteem.
- Students will understand that caring for others is a responsibility of everyone in a civilized society.
- Students will develop ways to exhibit caring.

KEY CONCEPTS

Despite what the character Gordon Gekko, in the movie Wall Street, said, greed (and selfishness) is not good. If everyone believed that "it's every man for himself," cities would never be built, and societies would never evolve past the hunter–gatherer stage.

MATERIALS NEEDED

Fake, board game–type money, preferably in thousand-dollar denominations

POSSIBLE OPTIONAL DISCUSSION TOPICS

Empathy is an underrated trait. In the famous book and movie *To Kill a Mockingbird,* Atticus Finch says to his daughter, "You never fully understand a person until you…climb inside his skin and walk around in it." (Lee, 1960). Discuss what that means.

ACTIVITY—THE BILLIONAIRE PHILANTHROPIST GAME INSTRUCTIONS

- Marco is a millionaire who learned that money isn't everything. It's time for your students to play "Millionaire." In this activity, students will have $10,000 in play money to spend.
- The catch is they cannot spend it on themselves. They must spend it on others or on nonprofit organizations. Students will take turns going around the room announcing how they will give away their money (e.g., "$1,000 to…" regarding what influenced their choices will follow).

BACKGROUND

You may recognize the character of Tempus's alter ego because he is almost an archetype of the spoiled brat billionaire boy. Meet Max Marconi. His father made billions with forays into venture capitalism and by selling supercolliders (and sometimes weapons) to various governments. Max had everything going for him, including a nice spending allowance from Daddy, which he could spend on fancy clothes and fast cars. On top of that, he thought that he would eventually inherit all of his father's money and never have to work a day in his life.

That all changed when Argo gave him his power because he learned that there were things more powerful than money, and one of them was time.

You see, Max Marconi's power (and yes, I created name him after another personal hero—Italian inventor Guglielmo Marconi) as Tempus is limited time travel. Although Argo knew that this was a power that was potentially dangerous in the wrong hands (especially if one did something to alter the course of history), he gave it to someone like Max because he wanted to teach him some humility.

Tempus can only travel through time within the limits of his own life span. Once he figures this out, it becomes very sobering for him. If you knew exactly when you were going to die, it would give you pause as well.

While developing his time-travel skills, Tempus accidentally transports himself to some of the darkest times and some of the deadliest places. Among other things, he saw firsthand famine in Africa and genocide and war in the Middle East. He knew if his father's supercolliders fell into the hands of someone who wanted to weaponize them, what destruction would follow.

Much like military veterans that experience posttraumatic stress, Max was changed after he saw the horrors of war and poverty up close. He changed his ways. He became more caring and concerned for his fellow man. He became less self-centered. He mounted a crusade to make the world a better place and urged his father to become a philanthropist.

As one of the Essentialz, Tempus knows that he always must exercise care to not impact history or established timelines. Tempus cares about his teammates so much and has become so selfless that he will often risk his own life to keep them safe.

Caring is one of the cornerstones of character education because it teaches our students empathy.

If our students are more compassionate, they are more likely to show respect. If they are empathetic, they are less likely to bully others or discriminate.

Refer back to the accompanying slide show presentation associated with this chapter.

DISCUSSION

- How selfless are you?
- Do you think about the feelings and needs of others first before yourself?
- Can you be better at being charitable?
- Remember: Ripples in a Pond!

16

Sparks and Leadership

LENGTH OF LESSON

30 to 35 minutes

LEARNING OBJECTIVES

- Students will recognize that there is more to leadership than likeability.
- Students will understand the qualities of a good leader.

KEY CONCEPTS

Leadership is just as important to an advanced society as cooperation is. We need leaders to help us prioritize and follow a plan. Good leaders help groups, teams, countries, and so on, succeed and prosper. Bad leaders lead them to failure and in the worst cases, even extinction, so learning the characteristics of a good leader should be pretty important.

MATERIALS NEEDED

One or two old area rugs

POSSIBLE OPTIONAL DISCUSSION TOPICS

There are many different styles of leadership. Discuss the difference between micromanaging teachers/coaches and more laid-back ones. Can more than one style be effective?

ACTIVITY—THE SURVIVOR RUG CHALLENGE GAME

- Sparks is a quiet leader. However, in this activity a leader will have to speak up. In the Survivor Rug Challenge Game, the group will be broken up into teams, and a leader for each team is selected randomly. Then, each team will stand on an area rug.
- The teams can take turns or if you have more than one rug, each team can stand on its own rug simultaneously. The counselor will instruct teams that they are to turn over the rug while standing on it, BUT they must also imagine that anywhere off of the rug is like lava or on fire. Therefore, they must not step off the rug while turning it over, or else they lose. The leader must give the directions for moving the other members and turning over the carpet. The fastest team wins.
- A discussion will follow about what type of leadership style was most effective.

BACKGROUND

Our last Bunsen hero is Sparks. His alter ego is Blaise Rogers. His last name is my homage to American psychologist Carl Rogers. While Blaise is fascinated with physics and electricity, he is just as interested in the behavioral sciences such as psychology.

One of Blaise's heroes is Nikola Tesla. Blaise convinced his friends Fuega and Tempus to help him build a Tesla energy coil in his garage. Little did he know that by using unconventional parts, which Max commandeered from Marconi Industries, he would draw the attention of Argo and facilitate a portal between this world and Argo's Zetaverse.

Argo's gift to Blaise is the ability to control electricity. As Sparks, small static jolts to powerful bolts of lightning can emanate from his hands. Besides that, Sparks has enhanced axon control of his brain cells, which means that while he was smart before, when he transformed into Sparks, he became a super-genius and could process information faster than a computer.

In the Essentialz story, Sparks is not only the leader of the Bunsens; he eventually becomes the leader of all the Essentialz. You see, in the fictional world of my creation at least, intelligence wins out over brawn, money, and even super-patriotism.

I thought that it was important to teach our kids about the elements (see what I did there?) of good leadership, especially when it seems like our world doesn't always present us with shining examples. So, I created Sparks with the ideal qualities of a good leader: Sparks has a vision, he has focus, he listens to others, he is fair, he is humble, he knows how to delegate jobs, he is a cheerleader for the team, and he doesn't micromanage.

In the end, I review with my students that not everybody can be a leader because not everyone wants to be or is cut out for the job. However, if you want to be a true leader, don't be a bully, don't be negative, be open to other opinions, and understand that a leader is a servant. Finally, surround yourself with talented, competent people. Stay the heck out of their way, and let them do what they do best!

Refer back to the accompanying slide show presentation associated with this chapter.

DISCUSSION

- What quality in a person makes you want to follow them? Is it more than just "likeability?
- Do you think you have the qualities to be a leader?
- What are the challenges of being the leader?
- What does it mean to "lead by example?"

17

Female Comic Book Heroes and Stereotypes

LENGTH OF LESSON

30 to 35 minutes

LEARNING OBJECTIVES

- Students will recognize that women have made many accomplishments in all areas of society, entertainment, science, exploration, business, advocacy, and government.
- Students will understand the importance of gender equality.

KEY CONCEPTS

For centuries, men ran the world and women were either subservient or were treated like second-class citizens. They were exploited, marginalized, or had their rights abridged. Fortunately, those times are over. The "glass ceiling" is broken and the world is learning that women can do anything from leading Fortune 500 companies to leading countries and finding cures for cancer. Furthermore, when women are free to contribute, all of society benefits.

MATERIALS NEEDED

Printouts of Bingo cards provided in Appendix A, Bingo clues also provided in Appendix A

POSSIBLE OPTIONAL DISCUSSION TOPICS

Does Hollywood and the media in general focus too much attention on the perfect body image? Do we feel pressure to have the perfect body, toned muscles or compare our physical development to others?

ACTIVITY

- To enlighten students of the accomplishments of women, you can play Girl Power Bingo. Using the Bingo cards template provided in Appendix A, break up the class into groups. Each group gets a Bingo card.
- The counselor will call out clues that are accomplishments of famous women (a list of possible clues is also available in Appendix A).
- The students will mark off the names on the Bingo card until one team has a straight or diagonal line marked off, just like in traditional Bingo.

BACKGROUND

In the comedy genre, the 'segue' is your best friend. Many of the consecutive lessons dovetail right into each other, such as Fisk, and Overcoming Disabilities segues into Fisk and Overcoming Discrimination. Any of the female Essentialz lessons can segue into a lesson about gender discrimination.

This is a very fertile topic for so many reason and opens up a veritable plethora of talking points with female students (and male students, too), especially middle schoolers. Shattering stereotypes, gender-based discrimination in hiring, body image issues, and even objectification of women are all subjects you can address with this lesson.

Sana Amanat is an editor at Marvel and one of the most influential women in the comic book industry. Not only is she a champion of women's rights; she is a staunch believer in comic books as a vehicle for empowering young women.

Female comic book heroines today shatter the stereotype that only men can save the world. The message here is clear: women can do anything men can do.

Unfortunately, one of the things that women like Sana have to crusade against in the comic world is that many of these female characters have perfect or even exaggeratedly endowed bodies. This leaves them open to being potential sex objects for male readers and could potentially perpetuate another stereotype: the need for women to have a perfect body.

Mind you, males envy the washboard abs of their comic book heroes, but many experts on adolescents feel females are especially sensitive to the fact that one or more of their body parts are not exactly the way they want.

To that end, at the urging of executives like Sana, comic books are doing a better job of portraying female superheroes with more realistic body proportions. Also, other female superheroes are getting costume makeovers so that their uniforms are less revealing and skintight.

For this lesson's slides, I don't plaster them with text. I keep it simple, leave it open ended, and encourage my students to give me their opinions on the way women are portrayed in all types of media, and to a greater extent how they are portrayed in our Western society. You might even want to open a discussion on how women are portrayed in other cultures and societies. Is ours better or worse in their eyes?

Another important conversation that you can have with your students can be about preventing violence against women. Even though the comics depict our superheroines as being tough and able to handle themselves in a fight, the reality of life is that women are rarely more physically imposing than men. Therefore, it is important to discuss with our male students that it is never acceptable to hit or get physically aggressive with a woman, and our female students need to hear that it is never okay to be hit by a man. Today's headlines are full of incidents where our students' entertainment and sports role models have been charged with physically abusing women. One idea I had in mind when creating the Essentialz was that heroes should not only fight supervillains but should also be instrumental in fighting social issues like domestic violence as well.

Refer back to the accompanying slide show presentation associated with this chapter.

DISCUSSION

- Even though super-heroines are tough, in real life, it is still NEVER okay to hit a girl.
- Super-heroines might get less recognition for doing the same job as male heroes. Sometimes women get paid less than men for doing the same job. Is that fair?
- Do you think women heroes in comic books are sometimes taken less seriously because of the way they are dressed?

18

The Essentialz and Teamwork

LENGTH OF LESSON

30 to 35 minutes

LEARNING OBJECTIVES

- Students will recognize the power of teamwork versus trying to do everything on their own.
- Students will understand that effective groups (and even well-functioning families) compromise and find ways to get along, even if they do not all like each other.

KEY CONCEPTS

Learning how to function in a group is not only an essential school and business skill, it could one day be a survival skill.

MATERIALS NEEDED

Bag of large marshmallows, paper tape, box of spaghetti or popsicle sticks, string

POSSIBLE OPTIONAL DISCUSSION TOPICS

What is social loafing? What happens when only a few members of a group do all the work and some don't do anything but share in the credit?

ACTIVITY—THE TOWER CHALLENGE GAME INSTRUCTIONS

- Divide the class into groups.
- Each group is provided the above materials, and they must build the tallest freestanding tower of marshmallows possible.
- The tallest tower wins.

BACKGROUND

Lately, the writers of comics do a great job of fleshing out story lines that play up group dynamics. These plot lines find their way into comic book–related movies as well, and they are great teachable moments for our kids. That's why I thought it was important to develop these themes even more when I created the Essentialz. My story lines include poignant, dramatic character interpersonal dynamics such as initial mistrust, bonding, friendship, infighting, and implicit trust.

Any time they are on a sports team, choir, school play, or even a group project, our students are going to encounter the group dynamics mentioned above. So, if one of our goals is to help create socially and emotionally competent kids, it is particularly important to teach them that teams and other groups are often like families—they bicker and fight but eventually get over it for the good of the group. Not only will this lesson make adolescence smoother for them, but it will also provide invaluable social practice that lends itself to achieving success in adulthood.

Refer back to the accompanying slide show presentation associated with this chapter.

DISCUSSION

- TEAMWORK makes a dream work!
- Have you ever been part of a team?
- Were you ever involved in a group project?

- Did you do your part?
- Could the others depend on you?
- Do you think that your friends would describe you as dependable?

19

Real-Life Superheroes from History

LENGTH OF LESSON

20 to 25 minutes

LEARNING OBJECTIVES

- Students will understand that looking up to our heroes is more valuable when it is based in reality.
- Students will recognize that history is full of inspirational stories of people doing heroic things.

KEY CONCEPTS

Superhero stories are fun, but they are fantasy. Students can draw inspiration from real-life events by visiting the biography and history sections of the library as much as they can in the fiction section.

MATERIALS NEEDED

A library card. Encourage your students to read about their favorite historical figures and decide for themselves if they are worthy role models.

POSSIBLE OPTIONAL DISCUSSION TOPICS

Is there a famous historical figure—a president, actor, author, activist, etc. who you have read/heard about who you think of as a hero?

ACTIVITY

- Go to the library.
- Read about your favorite person from history.
- Find out what makes them so super!

BACKGROUND

We have just spent the last fifteen sessions expending a lot of energy showing our students that the Essentialz are great role models, but there is just one problem with them: they aren't real.

As I mentioned before, our kids love to read about and watch superheroes in part because they want to escape reality and their mundane or even unsavory lives, but now it is time to bring them back to Earth.

This lesson is a great opportunity for cross-curriculum learning. In this session, we are going to introduce famous figures throughout history and reflect on how some of their accomplishments exemplify good character traits. In my initial treatment of the subject, I simply plucked a few people off the top of my head and plugged them into the discussion, so what I use in this slide presentation is far from a complete list. There are literally hundreds of examples of people that you can find throughout the history of man, both ancient and recent American history that you can use to customize your own discussions.

The ones that I chose were Sally Ride and bravery, Abraham Lincoln and honesty, Rosa Parks and battling discrimination, Gandhi and peaceful protest, Sir Ernest Shackleton and determination.

I always include John F. Kennedy in this presentation as a nod to the part he played in the inspiration of my book, and this chapter in particular. Way back when I was in eighth grade, my sister got married, and when she moved out, she left behind a book she had read in high school—*Profiles in Courage* by John F. Kennedy. I picked it up, and I was hooked after the first chapter. My lifelong passion for good character had begun.

In 1957, JFK won a Pulitzer Prize for writing *Profiles in Courage,* which is a volume of short biographies of United States senators such as John Quincy Adams, Daniel Webster, and Sam Houston. They exhibited great courage while serving their country and constituents by standing up for what was right and for sticking to their convictions.

Throughout this program, I've encouraged you to have fun with the topics in this series. For this particular week, I'm going to encourage you to do what I did: make it as personal as possible. Feel free to use your favorite role models from history, or just simply use the ones I have provided if you like them. The choice is up to you, but I have learned that if you use examples of people who are your personal heroes or someone you have a strong admiration for, the kids can really sense that.

Practically everyone knows the story of "Honest Abe" Lincoln who, as a young man working in a general store, allegedly walked several miles to give the correct change to a customer he had overcharged. The veracity of this story is always debatable because it was used during his political campaigns, but it does show that at one time at least in the history of this country, honesty was a valued virtue.

Sally Ride exhibited incredible courage by being the first American woman in space aboard the Space Shuttle Challenger. Plenty of things can go wrong on a NASA mission, but she faced the risks unflinchingly in order to blaze new trails for women and science. She showed even greater bravery in her later life when she battled pancreatic cancer, a battle she eventually lost.

In 1955, there were "Jim Crow" laws in the state of Alabama which segregated white and black people in public places. One statute ordered that white people were entitled to the preferred seats in the front of public transportation vehicles like busses and black people were relegated to the back. One day, Rosa Parks was ordered by a bus driver to give up her seat in the "colored" section to a white woman when the white section was full. Rosa refused, which sparked a boycott of public transportation in Montgomery and eventually effected changes in civil rights in the United States.

One of my personal favorites is Sir Ernest Shackleton, who mounted several expeditions to the South Pole. On one trip, he attempted to cross Antarctica from sea to sea, but his ship (appropriately named the *Endurance*) was trapped in the ice, and he had to lead an escape of his crew via a voyage of over 700 nautical miles in lifeboats.

To simplify the story of Mohandas Gandhi, he was a lawyer and congressman in India. After years of oppression, Gandhi felt that the British rule in his nation was wrong and oppressive. In 1920, he mounted a civil disobedience protest among Indians that employed nonviolent non-cooperation that eventually led to Indian independence from England.

Finally, one of my absolute favorite examples is an emotional and poignant story and one to which I make a personal connection: the story of Pat Tillman. Football has been a major part of my life. Growing up near Philadelphia, I was and still am a huge Eagles fan. I detested Pat Tillman, an Arizona Cardinal player, at first, but I grew to have incredible respect for his gutsy game and his hustle.

I had even greater respect for his life off the field. After September 11, 2001, Pat was so upset by the thought that America was attacked in such a cowardly way, that he quit the NFL and started the grueling task of becoming a U.S. Army Ranger. As an NFL player, he was doing something he loved; he was getting recognition at it and he was making good money.

He turned down a 3.6 million dollar contract over 3 years from the Cardinals in order to join the Army with his brother and did several tours in Afghanistan. This feel-good story became an American tragedy when Pat was killed by friendly fire during the war, but it exemplifies his courage in that he was willing to give up a cushy life and make the ultimate sacrifice to fight for his country. For that, I believe Pat is a real-life superhero.

Refer back to the accompanying slide show presentation associated with this chapter.

20

Everyday Heroes

LENGTH OF LESSON

20 to 25 minutes

LEARNING OBJECTIVES

- Students will understand that real-life heroes don't have to be historical figures.
- Students will recognize that we should appreciate the people in our lives that make sacrifices every day to help us or keep us safe.

KEY CONCEPTS

Appreciation for altruism. There are examples all around us of people who are heroic because they go out of their way to help others. If we were all bankers, entertainers, or professional athletes, who would keep our streets safe, keep us healthy, or teach us how to read?

MATERIALS NEEDED

There are no materials needed; this is an opportunity for honest discussion.

POSSIBLE OPTIONAL DISCUSSION TOPICS

Do you know someone who has done something extraordinary to help someone else in need? Have you, yourself, ever reached out to help or inspire someone else?

ACTIVITY

- Generate an honest discussion on what it means to each participant to be a hero.
- Being a hero means doing the right thing, whether it's convenient or not, whether it's popular or not. Being a hero also means doing the right thing, even if NO ONE is watching

BACKGROUND

Here is our road map so far. First, we validated for our students that reading is indeed cool. Next, we showed them that one of the things that makes fictional characters such as the Essentialz worthy of their admiration is that these heroes exemplify several good character traits; then we showed them that the Essentialz face the same kinds of challenges (such as anxiety, anger, and intolerance) that they do but still manage to make the right choices because of their integrity and good character. We brought the students back to reality by showing them that certain historic figures are even more worthy of our fandom and admiration than fictional heroes because they actually lived through challenging and crucial situations and prevailed, due in no small part to their impeccable character.

Now, we are going to bring it home for our students and make it very real for them by pointing out modern, real-life people that they may see every day that do heroic things in the completion of their jobs.

To their credit, modern media does not do a bad job of highlighting the importance of our armed service people and our veterans. I am particularly attuned to this because the name of the school that I work in is dedicated to the sacrifice of our veterans, and we refer to this all of the time in our presentations and character activities. However, for kids in other schools, the message of those U.S. Military commercials may get lost in all the background noise.

Prime-time television is full of serial dramas that feature the important work of doctors, police detectives, fire fighters, and EMTs. Unfortunately, most of our students aren't choosing those shows. They are often watching media that have little redeeming value.

Just as sad is the fact that there aren't enough TV shows about the importance of teachers in my opinion, either.

So, this week's slide show, the wrap-up session, is where we highlight the valor of the Army, Navy, Air Force, Marines, and Coast Guard.

We review the fact that doctors, fire fighters, and EMTs save lives every day.

Lately, our police personnel throughout the country are being scrutinized. In reality, they keep us safe, prevent crimes, save lives, and the vast majority of them are honest and do a great job under very challenging conditions. It's our job as educators to encourage our students to be law-abiding and to respect all law-enforcement officers.

It's also time to toot our own horns as well. I'm obviously preaching to the choir here, but I believe that teachers deserve recognition as heroes, too. In our school, we have t-shirts for our staff that say, "I teach. What's your superpower?"

But why stop there? What about the counselors, nurses, crossing guards, security guards, and custodians in our school? They deserve the respect and admiration of our students as well.

Again, this is another session that you can customize to your particular school and make personal for you. I don't have many words on this week's slides, because the ideas are pretty self-evident, and this is meant to be a session that is very, very discussion-driven.

> *Refer back to the accompanying slide show presentation associated with this chapter.*

21

Making the Final Connection—Kids Can Be Super

A word of advice: never consider the program as a perfect, finished product. Keep on working to improve it. The very first version of the presentation that I showed to my students was far from flawless. Originally, I wanted to show them that anyone could step up to the plate and do something borderline heroic and beyond their comfort level, so that when life called upon them, they knew that even they could do it. So, I used myself as an example in an incident that happened to me in 2010.

My friends and I helped people in a car accident and after the police arrived, we filled them in on the details. We left before the news reporters got there (it was late, and we were tired).

I thought it was a good story with a lot of good talking points. I was proud of the way my wife and friends jumped into action. We made the right choice by not shrugging it off as "not our problem" and driving away. We did not do it for the recognition from the media (as I said, we left long before TV crews arrived). We did not do it to receive any kind of thanks. It was the right thing to do in a time of need.

However, here is where I was wrong: I should not have used myself as an example. As much as I had good intentions with ending the series this way, it smacks of arrogance, and it sends the wrong message to our students.

Instead, end your presentation with this: search the Internet for a story (preferably one with pictures) of a real-life teen that did something heroic. You would be surprised how many stories there are out there-kids can really amaze you!

When I was younger, I was a cub scout. As a scout you get a free automatic subscription to the monthly magazine, *Boys' Life*. The magazine is still in existence, but they have ceased one recurring piece that I believe was very important: the final page of each issue of the magazine always featured a realistic cartoon dramatization of the story of a real-life boy scout who acted quickly and courageously to save a life.

Those stories really affected me. I always daydreamed about if an emergency happened, would I be ready? Would I be prepared? I vowed that if I were ever in that situation, I would not freeze or panic. I would act decisively. I like to think that *Boys' Life* helped to prepare me for that moment in August of 2010.

So, I suggest that instead of ending the presentation series with my story or your own personal story, or any story of an adult, end it with something remarkably courageous that a peer (preferably, a local one) did in real life. Who knows? Perhaps by ending the slide show with something that our kids can really connect with emotionally it might continue the *Boys' Life* tradition of inspiring even more real-life heroes.

To prove just how easy it is to come up with such examples, I just Googled "teens that acted heroically" and got back the following: a 2013 article from online magazine *The Week* (Hansen, 2013) that provided details of nine recent events (as reported by major newspapers such as *The Sun-Sentinel, Detroit Free Press,* and *The Oregonian*) where teens saved lives, including:

1. The prom-bound teens that came to the aid of car-crash victims.
2. The high school baseball team that lifted a car to save a life.

3. The 14-year-old who protected a rape victim from her assailant.
4. The 14-year-old who saved a young boy from a burning building.
5. The 16-year-old who braved thin ice to save a boy from drowning.
6. The 16-year-old who saved his fellow campers during a bear attack.
7. The 18-year-old who pulled the driver out of a truck hanging off a cliff.
8. The teen that saved his South Dakota school from a Columbine-like tragedy.
9. The 14-year-old who saved two men from drowning.

> *Refer back to the accompanying slide show presentation associated with this chapter.*

Here is another bonus that I just learned about that could also be your last presentation and impetus for your students to keep the spirit of heroic deeds going throughout the year.

You could call this chapter, "Huck and Altruism"

Image Comics is an up-and-coming publisher. Their comic book series include *Spawn* (1992), *Witchblade* (1995), and *The Walking Dead* (2003). One of their most celebrated writers, Mark Millar, has penned some pretty famous series in his time including ones that have been turned into blockbuster movies.

Mark decided to create a new character for Image Comics called simply, Huck, and launched it in July of 2016.

Here is Image's description of Huck:

"In a quiet seaside town, a gas station clerk named Huck secretly uses his special gifts to do a good deed each day. When his story leaks, a media firestorm erupts, bringing him uninvited fame. As pieces of Huck's past begin to resurface, it's no longer clear who his friends are—or whose lives may be in danger."

Huck, it seems, is a gentle giant of a young man with unusual strength and special abilities who understands the intrinsic satisfaction of helping others. No masks, no capes, no secret identity; just one individual trying to make the lives of others better. Mark Millar calls it the true essence of a superhero.

Finally, it seems, comic book publishers are starting to understand the power of their influence on our kids!

On Mark Millar's Twitter account (@MarkMillar), he encouraged people to be more like Huck and do one good deed a day. This inspired a worldwide trending for the Twitter tag #onegooddeed and another Twitter account was spawned called The Huck Challenge (@HuckChallenge), which offers a place for people to post their one good deed for the day and to challenge their friends to do one as well.

This is a great way to get your students excited about altruism and doing good deeds in the real world.

22

Expanding the Program

Hopefully, you will have as much fun as your students will with this subject matter. Beyond just having fun, though, is the real hope that your kids will be more receptive to the message of good character, embrace it, and even internalize it into their personalities for a lifetime.

One way of increasing the odds of that happening is to extend that message beyond your counseling area or classroom. I am very fortunate to have an awesome principal and administrative team that gave me the green light to really go for it. I was able to buy street signs for the hallways of my school that reminded the students of the lessons we gave them: Responsibility Road, Honesty Heights, Trustworthy Terrace, Kindness Court, and Hall of Heroes (our glass display case that honored veterans with pictures and biographies), etc. The staff really began to buy into the idea when we asked them to vote on these names. We were also blessed with a superintendent that believes strongly in technology, so we have flat-panel TVs in the classrooms and some hallways, too. I was able to broadcast a different superhero slide every week that reminded the students of what they learned in the presentation: A certain webslinger, by my design, with the caption, "Superpowers require super responsibility." A certain super guy and the caption, "There is real strength in kindness." A certain 'wonderful' woman and the inscription saying, "Defy stereotypes."

Here's another reality: as much fun as the program can be, it has a definite shelf life. You can't repeat it year after year without boredom setting in or compromising its effectiveness. There is the potential for the program to get stale. I encourage you to change things up the next school year.

In other publications, I will show you how to do the same thing as this character education program, only using clips from G and PG-rated Hollywood movies. In the meantime, go out there and enjoy being 'super' for your students.

Appendix A

Super Women

GIRL POWER BINGO

B	I	N	G	O
Marie Curie	Indira Gandhi	Susan B. Anthony	Harriet Tubman	Gloria Steinem
Princess Diana	Sally Ride	Beyoncé	J.K. Rowling	Mary Lou Retton
Kerri Walsh	Lady Gaga	**FREE SPOT**	Frida Kahlo	Lucille Ball
Meryl Streep	Joan of Arc	Jane Goodall	Oprah Winfrey	Amelia Earhart
Jane Austen	Mother Teresa	Hillary Clinton	Vera Wang	Helen Keller

GIRL POWER BINGO

B	I	N	G	O
Lady Gaga	Lucille Ball	Joan of Arc	Mother Teresa	Hillary Clinton
Susan B. Anthony	Gloria Steinem	Amelia Earhart	Beyoncé	Kerri Walsh
J.K. Rowling	Oprah Winfrey	**FREE SPOT**	Jane Goodall	Sally Ride
Mary Lou Retton	Helen Keller	Princess Diana	Marie Curie	Indira Gandhi
Harriet Tubman	Frida Kahlo	Vera Wang	Meryl Streep	Jane Austen

GIRL POWER BINGO

B	I	N	G	O
Harriet Tubman	Marie Curie	Jane Goodall	Gloria Steinem	Indira Gandhi
J.K. Rowling	Princess Diana	Hillary Clinton	Mary Lou Retton	Sally Ride
Frida Kahlo	Kerri Walsh	**FREE SPOT**	Lucille Ball	Lady Gaga
Oprah Winfrey	Meryl Streep	Susan B. Anthony	Amelia Earhart	Joan of Arc
Vera Wang	Jane Austen	Beyoncé	Helen Keller	Mother Teresa

GIRL POWER BINGO

B	I	N	G	O
Mary Lou Retton	Oprah Winfrey	Princess Diana	Jane Goodall	Kerri Walsh
Harriet Tubman	Helen Keller	Vera Wang	Marie Curie	Sally Ride
Hillary Clinton	Frida Kahlo	**FREE SPOT**	Meryl Streep	Indira Gandhi
Susan B. Anthony	Lucille Ball	Joan of Arc	Mother Teresa	Jane Austen
J. K. Rowling	Gloria Steinem	Amelia Earhart	Beyoncé	Lady Gaga

CLUES FOR GIRL POWER BINGO

1. This journalist was an editor at *Ms.* magazine and was instrumental in starting the Women's Liberation movement of the 1970s.
2. This woman was a member of British royalty known for her humanitarian work with AIDS patients and the homeless.
3. This astronaut was the first American woman in space.
4. This author was the creator of the *Harry Potter* series and rose from poverty to be one of the richest and most influential people in the literature world today.
5. This American spy was born a slave and created the Underground Railroad to help slaves escape to freedom during the Civil War.
6. This aviator was the first female pilot to fly solo across the Atlantic Ocean.
7. This political figure was the only female prime minister of India.
8. This woman led the women's suffrage movement in the late 1800s to win the right to vote for American women. She was the first woman commemorated on U.S. currency.
9. This athlete was the first American Olympian to win the gold medal in the individual all-around competition in gymnastics.
10. This French physicist was the first woman to win a Nobel Prize for her work on radioactive elements.
11. This beach volleyball Olympian has three gold medals and is the career leader in volleyball victories.
12. This Chinese-American fashionista is one of the most popular clothing designers in history.
13. This American politician is the only woman to go from first lady to winning her party's nomination for U.S. president and even winning the popular vote in the presidential election.
14. This comedienne won four Emmys for her work on TV sitcoms and is sometimes called "The First Lady of Comedy."
15. With hits like "Poker Face," "Bad Romance," and "Born This Way," this singer/songwriter/actress is a cultural icon.

16. This singer was the leader of Destiny's Child, but her stardom really took off when she went solo with songs like "Single Ladies."
17. This French woman was a fierce warrior and is considered a saint in the Catholic church.
18. She is one of the most recognized TV personalities. She started her own network and is one of the richest women in the world as a result of decades as a talk-show host.
19. This fearless zoologist studied the social life of apes in their natural habitat.
20. This Mexican artist was known for her striking self-portraits and feminism.
21. Despite being deaf and blind, this woman became an author, and her life and struggles were made into books and movies.
22. This woman was canonized as a saint by her religion and was recognized for her charitable work in India, especially Calcutta.
23. This American performer was nominated for more Academy Awards (Oscars) than any other actor or actress.
24. This British woman wrote several books, including *Sense and Sensibility*, cleverly describing the social life of her times.

References

Bandura, A., Ross, D., & Ross, S. A. (1961). Transmission of aggression through the imitation of aggressive models. *Journal of Abnormal and Social Psychology, 63*(3), 575–582.

Blad, E. (2015). *Survey: Student Success Calls for More Than Academic Skills*. Retrieved from Education Week: http://www.edweek.org/ew/articles/2015/06/10/survey-student-success-calls-for-more-than.html

Brevoort, T. (personal communication, August, 2015).

Cicchini, P. (2019). *The Essentialz.* Grapevine, TX: Waldorf Publishing.

Clark, E. (2012). *Why Kids Love Superheroes*. Retrieved May, 2012 from http://www.savvysource.com

Charactercounts.org (1992). Six Pillars of Character® (per the Aspen Declaration) .

Crichton, M. (Director). (1973). *Westworld* [Motion Picture].

Freud, S. (1914). *On Narcissim: an Introduction.* Freiburg, Germany: White Press.

Hansen, L. (2013). *9 heroic teens and their incredible acts of bravery [Updated]*. Retrieved from The Week: http://theweek.com/articles/468498/9-heroic-teens-incredible-acts-bravery-updated

Hugo, V. (1862). *Les Miserables.* New York, NY: Washington Square Press.

Josephson Institute. (2007). *Effectiveness of Character Counts-Evidence Based Results*. Retrieved from https://charactercounts.org/program-overview/results

Kirkman, Robert (Writer). Moore, T. (Artist). Adlard, C. (Artist). (2003). *The Walking Dead.* [Comic Book]. Cynthiana, KY: Image Comics.

Lee, H. (1960). *To Kill a Mockingbird.* New York, NY: J.B. Lippincott & Co.

Lickona, T. (2004). *Character Matters: How to Help Our Children Develop Good Judgment, Integrity, and Other Essential Virtues* (chapter), New York, NY: Atria Books.

Lickona, T. E. (1994). *Eleven principles of effective character education.* Washington, D.C.: Character Education Partnership.

MacDonald, H. (2016, August 16). *The Beat.* Retrieved from https://www.comicsbeat.com/marvel-40-of-our-readers-are-female-and-our-sales-are-just-fine-thanks

McFarlane, T. (Creator) & DeFalco, T. (Contributor) (1992). *Spawn* [Comic Book], Detroit, MI: Image Comics.

Millar, Mark (2016) *Huck.* [Comic Book]. Portand, OR: Image Comics.

Ostroff, J. (2014, August 28). *Why Your Kids Love Super Heroes (and Why You Should Take Them to Comic-Cons).* Retrieved from https://www.huffingtonpost.ca/joshua-ostroff/comic-cons-fan-expo_b_5725322.html

Payton, J. W. (2008). The positive impact of social and emotional learning for kindergarten to eighth-grade students: Findings from three scientific reviews. Chicago, IL: Collaborative for Academic, Social, and Emotional Learning (CASEL).

Saunders, B (2011). *Do the Gods Wear Capes? Spirituality, Fantasy, and Superheroes*. New York, NY: Continuum Publishing Corporation.

Shapiro, B. (2011). *Why Do We Love Superheroes?* Retrieved from http://www.frontpagemag.com/fpm/93068/why-do-we-love-superheroes-ben-shapiro

Silvestri, M (Creator) Stampfl, T. G., & Levis, D.J. (1967). Essentials of implosive therapy: A learning-theory-based psychodynamic behavioral therapy. *Journal of Abnormal Psychology*, 72(6), 496-503.

U.S. Department of Education (2002). Retrieved from https://www2.ed.gov/admins/lead/character/brochure.html

Kirkman, R. (Founder and Owner). Moore, T. (Artist). Wohl, D. (Editor). Haberlin, B. (Writer). Z, Christina (Writer). Turner, M. (Artist). (1995). *Witchblade* [Comic Book]. New York, NY: Top Cow Productions, an imprint of Image Comics.

Wootton, J. M., Frick, P. J., Shelton, K. K., & Silverthorn, P. (1997). Ineffective parenting and childhood conduct problems: the moderating role of callous-unemotional traits. *Journal of Consulting and Clinical Psychology 65*(2), 301–308.

About the Author

Paul Cicchini, Ed.S., NCSP, is a nationally-certified school psychologist, author, and Templar Knight. He specializes in Character Education and counseling behaviorally-challenged students in public schools in New Jersey. Paul was mentored by renowned Rutgers professor Dr. Maurice Elias, and is now one of the few school psychologists in the country to be certified in School Leadership/ Character Education.

Paul is the author of the novels *Young Cyrano, Godsmacked,* and *The Essentialz.* He always weaves Character Education into his stories so that while parents and school personnel approve, the kids are also entertained. His love of superheroes is what inspired him to write *The Essentialz* and to create this curriculum.

Paul mentions the code of knighthood in his character education work because he has firsthand knowledge of it. Chevalier (Sir) Paul Cicchini KCTJ has achieved the rank of Knights Commander in the Sovereign Military Order of the Temple of Jerusalem, USA/ Philadelphia Priory—also known as the Knights Templar.

Paul also has special knowledge of football from every aspect of the game: player, coach, college scout, and news journalist. At age 43, he was still playing semi-pro football in the Diamond Football League. He garnered media attention for being the oldest linebacker to ever be awarded Player of the Week status.

Paul's list of accomplishments include martial artist, semi-pro linebacker, high school football coach, college scout, public speaker, college professor, and officer in the Sovereign Military Order of the Temple of Jerusalem (Philadelphia Priory of the U.S. Templar Knights).